REMEMBER THIS
TITAN

REMEMBER THIS
TITAN
THE BILL YOAST STORY

LESSONS LEARNED FROM A CELEBRATED COACH'S JOURNEY

AS TOLD TO
STEVE SULLIVAN

TAYLOR TRADE PUBLISHING
Lanham • New York • Boulder • Toronto • Plymouth, UK

Published by Taylor Trade Publishing
An imprint of The Rowman & Littlefield Publishing Group, Inc.
4501 Forbes Boulevard, Suite 200, Lanham, Maryland 20706

Estover Road, Plymouth PL6 7PY, United Kingdom

Distributed by NATIONAL BOOK NETWORK

The hardback edition of this book was previously
cataloged by the Library of Congress as follows:
Yoast, Bill R.
Remember this Titan : the Bill Yoast story : lessons learned from a
celebrated coach's journey / as told to Steve Sullivan.—1st Taylor Trade
Pub. ed.
p. cm.
1. Yoast, Bill R. 2. Football coaches—United States—Biography.
3. Football—Coaching. I. Sullivan, Steven D. II. Title.
GV939.Y63A3 2005
796.332'092—dc22
[B]
2005048597
ISBN-13: 978-1-58979-278-4 (cloth : alk. paper)
ISBN-10: 1-58979-278-5 (cloth : alk. paper)
ISBN-13: 978-1-58979-336-1 (pbk. : alk. paper)
ISBN-10: 1-58979-336-6 (pbk. : alk. paper)

∞ ™ The paper used in this publication meets the minimum requirements
of American National Standard for Information Sciences—Permanence of
Paper for Printed Library Materials, ANSI/NISO Z39.48-1992.

Manufactured in the United States of America.

Dedication

Betty, Angela, Susan Gail, Bonnie, Sheryl, Dee Dee

Special Thanks

Charles Peers

CONTENTS

FOREWORD

You are about to enter the world of Bill Yoast, so buckle up. This journey is not for the meek. It is filled with heartache, heartbreak, and hairpin turns. From the very beginning Bill Yoast had it tough and as he navigated his environment it got tougher. Thankfully he was up for it.

For most of us, we are not prepared for many of life's challenges. We learn little about ourselves and others when we are on cruise control. As Bill Yoast points out, the most important lessons are learned when the riding gets rough. Through adversity the best stuff sticks. In hardship, character is built.

The author, Steve Sullivan, has captured the essence of what makes Bill Yoast different. There is not a word wasted. This story is about a man who knew from the very beginning that other people count the most.

We live in a time when heroes are quickly fading from view. Thankfully there are people like Bill Yoast who we can turn to for inspiration.

It was not the record-breaking achievements obtained on the gridiron that made this coach "A Titan to Remember." It was his ability to see and develop talents in those he touched. He possessed a quiet strength; an invisible power that awakened the spirit in others. Bill Yoast knew how to build people. He knew that success off the field mattered more than what happened between the hash marks.

Steve Sullivan tells it like it was and not the way it should have been. The mistakes, the pain, the doubt is there. Bill Yoast was ahead of his time in racial equality and behind the time in seeking personal glory. Because of Bill Yoast kids became better. Some became great.

We often look to find our heroes from their accomplishments during major world events. What we often fail to recognize is that it was probably a coach, often not even known, who helped shape the character, integrity, and courage of those men and women that went on to achieve so much.

The lessons chronicled in this book should be required reading for everyone that wants to make a contribution. The author will take you to the edge of the cliff, where the view is the best. And from that vantage point, you will see, feel, and remember why Bill Yoast has been called an American hero.

Richard Ardia

PROLOGUE

Gerry is dead. The statement landed like a thunderbolt. As I put the phone down, I reflected on the young man I had known for a decade. From the first moment he walked through my door, I knew he was something special. I wasn't sure why but deep in my gut I had a feeling that Gerry Bertier and I were cut from the same bolt of cloth. I felt from the beginning that we were going on a journey joined at the hip.

You might think that a forty-five year old man with five kids and a lot of dust behind him would not be so easily captivated by a teenager. I myself was not sure what it was about Gerry that made him so appealing. He was enthusiastic, smart, and funny, but then there are many young men that carry that profile. It had nothing to do with his extroverted persona or his athletic ability. It was much deeper than that. When I looked at Gerry Bertier, I saw a man who was going to accomplish something. You only had to share a little time with him to know that he cared about things that were much greater than himself. When you broke into a conversation with Bertier it wasn't a frivolous event. The man was large but the things he cared about were even bigger.

He was an original, in every way. He was a man who lived the values he embraced. In the world of Gerry Bertier, integrity was not a word but a lifestyle. In Gerry's universe, duty, honor, and country were the coins of the realm. Determination, loyalty, and devotion were his breakfast of champions. Gerry believed that kindness was its own reward. In his world, the goal was to give more than you got. He also believed that accountability was for everyone. And that made him tough, with a capital T. It wasn't his inclination. He just understood no one becomes better by taking the easy way out. If you tried, you and Gerry were going to the mat.

From a hospital bed he energized a community. We can thank him for his leadership, his commitment, and his caring. It was at the heart of everything he did. I miss Gerry Bertier. I regret that our friendship ended in an instant. I'm not sad though. Gerry may be gone, but his spirit is as alive as the day we met.

Over the years I've been queried about Gerry Bertier. I've been asked about the Titans. Each time a question is posed I'm teleported to another place. Sometimes the Titans appear but more often than not I find myself in an unknown zone looking for answers. The visions are not as vivid as they used to be but they are clear enough. In the distance I see a dirt road splitting into a fragmented maze. I hesitate not knowing which path is right for me. I make a choice. The journey continues. Another maze appears. Suddenly I'm on a freeway. Things are speeding up. A world I didn't know existed appears in the windshield. The image vanishes. I'm brought back to reality when someone hollers, "Hey Coach."

Forty-seven years they called me Coach. For more than four decades young men and women walked through my door. Looking back on it, I have a sense of pride in what I've accomplished. I attempted to do my best with whatever was thrown my way. Sometimes it worked and sometimes it didn't. I've been given credit when credit wasn't due and I've been the fall guy when I was ready for a pat on the back. On balance, I have no complaints. And now that I have reached the twilight of this life and reflected back on how I got here, one thing becomes apparent. Of the thousands of kids that came into my life, seldom did I ever give more than I got.

PREFACE

It was a lifetime ago but I remember the conversation as if it took place yesterday. I was watching an interview that showcased a weathered football coach recounting his career. In the course of the conversation numerous questions were posed, covering a variety of topics. Everything he said had an impact. I could picture his locker room sermons. I could see his team hanging on every word. His energy jumped through my television.

It was apparent why the coaching icon had a remarkable record of achievement. And while I was impressed by his analysis of all that football stuff, the response he gave to a query unrelated to football impacted me the most. The question had to do with life. He answered:

I've always learned more from failure than success. For me, failure has been a teacher. On occasions it has been a friend. And like a friend, it gave me the straight scoop. It was failure that exposed my shortcomings. Failure that told me I wasn't ready. And because there was nothing I hated worse than a "know it all," failure became the catalyst to succeed. No I don't fear failure; I embrace it because in the end, failure will make me better.

Intriguing thoughts coming from a man whose name

was synonymous with success. Was he kidding? At that stage in my coaching career I didn't have the answers. I wasn't secure enough to want anything other than success. I didn't understand that defeat was the price of admission. Without defeat there would be no victory.

As a thirty-five-year-old math teacher with a limited record of accomplishments, failure was a punch in the nose. It was a kick in the butt. Failure sapped my energy and made me feel diminished. Failure caused my shoulders to sag and my eyes to gaze south. I walked a little unsteadily after failure.

Embrace failure? Who was he kidding? Maybe the coach wasn't as smart as I thought. I came to the conclusion that anyone who would befriend losing was a masochist and probably a fool. Fifty years later I have a different opinion. It didn't come overnight. It's come as a result of getting roughed up more times than I can count. But, as I look back on it, I realize failure has never been fatal. And in virtually every situation failure was a temporary event.

Here I am. The bruises are gone. The scrapes have healed and I'm on a roll. Did you hear? They put me in a movie. And now someone has asked me to write a book. I've decided I will. Well that's not exactly correct. I've employed a surrogate to put the words on paper. The thoughts will be mine.

I have a long history with the man that will help me crystallize what I want to say. My association with him was interrupted for thirty-five years but, like all relationships founded on substance, it remains intact. He came back into my life after seeing the movie *Remember the Titans*. His reappearance occurred suddenly one morning after I returned from a walk on Bethany Beach. I heard the phone ring but tried to ignore it. I then realized it probably was a call from the long lost quarterback and captain of the Hammond High School football team. I hadn't seen or heard from him in thirty years. An image flashed. The pain returned. I had to answer the phone because I wanted an explanation.

I put the receiver to my ear and the voice that posed the question sounded no differently. "Hey Bill," he said. "How come you never let me throw the bomb?" I couldn't believe it. In keeping with what I remembered, Steve Sullivan was still on the attack. Experience had taught me how to deal with a guy like Steve. "How come you fumbled on the one inch line?"

Since that call our friendship has grown. And so when I decided to accommodate a publisher's request, I turned to him. He wasn't particularly gracious. It didn't bother me because I've come to recognize Steve is a straight-talking guy. He stated that everything important has already been said. He told me a million books are written each year. He warned me that writing is hard. He explained the frustration that comes with searching for answers that may not exist. He told me that rejection was the name of the game. He said that the peanut gallery was waiting to eat my lunch.

I asked him what I should do. He responded, "When do we start?"

FORGED BY FIRE

I'm no different than anyone. I'd like to believe I came from "royal stock," that blue is the color of blood in my veins. I can picture the ship anchored at a London dock. Paperboys shout the news. Carriages pull up. Women are carrying parasols and men are looking dandy. The purser reads the manifest. "Yoast," he calls. No reply. "Yoast," he hollers. No answer. "Yoast!" he bellows. Silence. Someone grabs his arm. "Check Germany."

Poof. The fantasy is gone. There are no Yoasts that sailed with the *Mayflower*. As best as I can discern, the Yoasts embarked from somewhere else and I suspect their accommodations were anything but accommodating. They probably slept on a hay pile somewhere between the cow manure and goat droppings. They woke up every morning with feathers in their ears.

FAST FORWARD

My ancestors landed in America, and I showed up later in Florence, Alabama. Nineteen twenty-four to be exact. They called the place Tin Can Hollow. I don't know if the name related to the architectural design of the tenements or the debris lying in the street. I guess it didn't matter. It was my home.

At the time I was too young to reflect on the pedigree of my gene pool. As far as I knew, the Yoasts were as good as anyone. A few years later, my impression began to change when my dad invited me to accompany him to the train station. He was going on a trip and wanted me to see him off. I said sure. I loved my dad.

An hour later as we approached the rail yard I could see a locomotive chugging down the track spitting a spray of steam. Behind it was a line of cars that seemed to stretch forever. I looked at my dad and could see the excitement in his eyes. He commanded me to stay put. I always did what he told me so I froze in place. Momentarily, he was sprinting toward the train. As it drew closer he threw his carpetbag through an opening and dove into the boxcar. He didn't look back. Tears filled my eyes as I realized hobo Yoast was on his way.

A few months later I was playing in the street and when I turned around there was my pop. A smile decorated his face. His arms opened and I ran into them. It was good to have him home. A couple weeks went by and a circus came to town. My dad scrounged a couple tickets and took me into a different world. I had the time of my life.

The next day we went back to meet some of the performers. As we walked around the tents we stumbled into a group of tumblers practicing a pyramid. My dad asked if he could play. They put him on the bottom and stepped all over him. I remember him laughing and joking. He held his own. I could see he was having the time of his life. Two days later when the circus left town my father did too. It was a turning point for me. I realized then that my dad believed responsibility was for others. Each time he departed I seemed to care less. So did my mom and my sister. I guess Bobbie and I understood having a hobo for a role model could be detrimental.

I got to a point where I didn't care that my dad was gone. Part of it had to do with the fact that I had a surrogate on the other side of the county. Incidentally, she was black. Mary was her name and cotton was her game. I met her in a field on a blistering morning. I'll never forget those southern summer days. There was no escape; even the shade burned.

As you go through life it's interesting what images remain fresh in your mind. For me, meeting Mary has remained a vivid encounter. If you know anything about cotton then you know you gotta get pickin' before the sun slaps you silly. It's an early morning thing that means you rise a few hours after the moon showed its face. At least I did because the cotton field where I was going lived in the boonies.

The only way to get there was walking. As I trudged along I wondered what I was going to encounter. I stopped and looked around. I determined I was five miles from the middle of nowhere. The blackness and sounds of animals scurrying about didn't bother me. The fact that I was about to meet a bunch of people I didn't know made me a little nervous. I knew my social skills had grown slower than my feet.

I wondered if I was lost. I continued to walk. I turned a corner and could see the glow of small fire. I heard some laughing in the distance. It surprised me. Why would anyone be laughing at that hour, in that place?

I figured I'd find out.

I was glad that my journey had ended in success. As the first rays of morning light broke the horizon, the pinkish hue illuminated a group of pickers standing in a circle. I walked up with a smile on my face and gave them my name. Given the look on the twenty-nine faces that stared back I detected that they weren't as happy to see me as I was to see them. A second later a small woman erupted from the huddle. "Morning Bill, I'm Mary. Some call me Aunt Mary," she said and then extended her hand. As I grabbed it she showed me a smile with four hundred teeth.

The conversation quickly got around to business. I told her I had never picked cotton but I was a quick study. I'm not sure it was the truth but I was in desperate need of a job. Circumstances had made me a breadwinner. She smiled again. "There isn't much to it Bill," she said. Pointing to the puffs of white she explained the objective was to get as many in the bag as fast as you could. It was all about speed she stated. Speed made the difference between a full stomach or an empty cupboard. Handing me my burlap sack she wished me luck. It didn't come to me until a long time later: There was only so much cotton in that field. My getting more might mean that she would get less. I guess she didn't care.

Day after day I worked those fields. Somewhere in the beginning I got a silver dollar. That was a lot of cash for a nine year old. My heart almost jumped out of my chest. It was the first money I had ever made. I put it in my palm and gazed at it for a long time. I placed it in my pocket. I pulled it out and peered at it again. I rubbed my fingers across its shiny surface. *Gosh* I thought. I'm a workingman. It felt good. Two hours later I handed that silver dollar over to my mom. That felt even better.

That cotton field was a great learning experience. I learned about hard work, respect, responsibility, generosity and kindness. I learned about things that mattered. Most of it came from Mary. She toiled all day and yet there was always a song in her throat. I guess that also meant there was one in her heart. The other workers were friendly enough but there was a distance. I understood why. I was white and they were black. In the south in 1936 that combination only worked on a piano. Then one day that changed.

In a rush to get out of the house and down to the field I'd forgotten my water. And this day was no day to be without H2O. By daybreak it was hot. Torrid was in transit. I had been in the field an hour and started to wilt. I was feeling mighty bad but I'd gotten tough working those fields. I would suck it up. I prayed I'd make it.

At the morning break the pickers assembled under a big oak tree. Sitting in a circle the bucket and dipper was brought out and passed around. When it came to me, all eyes watched my move. They knew that I had been told if you drank water from a black man's cup your lips would fall off. I grabbed the dipper and took my turn.

Almost instantly you could detect a transformation had taken place. I was no longer Bill Yoast: white man. I was just another human being trying to get through a lousy day. At the time I didn't recognize the implication of my action; years later I did. The significance of an act rests in the eyes of the beholder.

I survived that day and the miserable days that followed. I did notice that the harder I worked the better I got. Each time out I picked a little more cotton. I set a goal that I would pick a hundred pounds. I realized that was half of what Mary grabbed but for me it would be a record.

When picking ended we took our bags to the scale. Every day I was disappointed. One afternoon Mary came up and asked how I'd done. The look on my face told her everything.

"Here, Bill," she said and then stuffed half her cotton into my bag. I hit the hundred pounds and never looked back. I became a picking machine. That act of generosity has never been forgotten.

Mary had her own family to feed and yet that was less important than doing something nice for someone else.

When you're young, time has a way of creeping pretty slow. It doesn't help if every day is punctuated with plight. If you're poor, it seems you never get dealt a winning hand and joy can turn to grief on a dime.

We had nothing so anything my sister and I got was a thrill. One day my mom had saved $2.00 for the down payment on a bike. She brought it home on a bus and for a moment I felt as good as anyone. Between my sister and me we logged five hundred miles the first hour. A month later two men showed up because my mom missed her payment. They wanted it back. Bobbie and I held hands and watched them load it on the truck. We couldn't believe the only fun in our lives had just been repossessed. I'll never forget it. Standing there were two kids with tears streaming down their faces and two guys who didn't care.

It was not long after I lost my wheels that I started hanging with an ugly crowd. The ringleader of the Tin Can Hollow bad boys was a delinquent by the name of Raymond Tefteller. Like Mary, he taught me a few things too. Under Raymond's guidance I learned to lie, cheat, and steal. I became a troublemaker. We were everywhere and everywhere we went something nasty happened.

One day we found ourselves outside of town at a waterhole. Tefteller knew a local sharecropper brought his cow there to drink. He had a plan. Sitting next to us was a pile of rocks. As the farmer stood at the pond Raymond started bombarding him. The man asked for Tefteller to stop. Raymond said he would if he was given a penny. In those days a penny could buy something. The man hesitated and took a couple more hits. He pleaded for my pal to stop. Another hit.

If you're wondering why a grown man would allow himself to be extorted by a kid, it had to do with color. He was black and we were white. In a racist society, if you're on the visiting team, you keep a low profile. When a rock hit him in the head I had seen enough. I told Tefteller it was wrong. I yelled to stop. He threw again and I threw myself at him. After I pounded Raymond into submission I looked at the man.

To this day I've not forgotten the look on his face. I've seen that look since then. It is a look of profound sadness. It is a look that asks "why me?" It's a look that acknowledges you are held captive by injustice and there is no escape. I felt sorrow for that old man.

For the next few days my conscience ached. I despised the feeling. I found my way back to the waterhole and there they were. I approached the sharecropper but I had nothing to say. I stood in silence near him and his cow. I finally got the courage to speak. I told him I was sorry but he didn't seem to care. I told him if there was anything I could do to help, I would. There was no reply. As he walked away I walked with him. No words were spoken. About a quarter mile down the road he stopped and handed me the rope that went around his cow's neck. I guess that was his way of saying I'd been forgiven. The next day I decided it was time to make some new friends.

A week later Tefteller was involved in the burning down of a warehouse. I was nowhere around. Raymond was sent to reform school. Shortly thereafter he was beaten to death by one of his kind.

I dodged a bullet. I'm thankful that Raymond Tefteller came into my life early on because it taught me one of the most valuable lessons I have learned. The people you associate with will have a dramatic impact on who you become.

A month went by and my best buddy became a bad memory. One day I was walking down the street and passed the cutest girl I'd ever seen. I was too bashful to say anything. She walked by and I did an about face. I spit on my hands and groomed my hair. I ran my tongue across my teeth.

I figured if I followed her to where she was going I might gather enough courage to ask her name. A half a mile away she walked into the Central Baptist Church. I decided it was time to take up religion. They were happy to have me. It was a turning point. In that church I was surrounded by people who focused on the right stuff. Acy Evans taught me about integrity, giving, sharing, and committing. Those years at the Central Baptist Church were some of the best I've had. I also learned that when you hang with good people they will lift you up.

The years became a blur. Picking and learning. Learning and picking. Hanging around. We moved a lot and it was usually a day before the rent was due. At least six times a week I got to eat. I started to grow up. My pants got shorter and my shirt got tight.

Somewhere around fourteen, I looked in the mirror to see what was up. I scrutinized the scrawny image that looked back. I was hoping to be proud of what I saw but wasn't. Being a beanpole with one set of threads and holes in my shoes was not a smiling matter. I knew I came from the left side of the tracks and that was just one more reason to frown. I did have a couple of things going for me. My body worked and my brain did too. I took up sports. On the field I could run and jump with the best of them. And in the classroom, they knew my name.

My sophomore year at Coffee High School I earned a letter. It was a moment of pride and joy. It was a big deal. That letter told me I'd made the cut. It said I was okay. The next day all the jocks had their award sewn to a sweater. Mine still remained in my hand. I wished I had a sweater. When I got my letter I thought I'd made it to the in-crowd. Now I was back on the outside looking in. I wasn't the only one who knew it. One day I was asked into a teacher's office. She had a grin that covered her face. On her desk sat a box. She opened it and my eyes almost popped out of my head. Mrs. McDonald had bought me a sweater.* As a result I learned that generosity is a fuel that ignites relationships.

I don't know exactly when the light went on. One day I realized that sports and books were my way out. I developed a plan. Unfortunately it was short-circuited in my junior year. It was 1943 when I got the news. The letter read:

> *Dear Billy Boy,*
> *We want you!*
> *Love, Uncle Sammy*

I was drafted into the Army Air Corps and I was excited. I wanted to serve my country but I also had another motive. I'd gotten tired of being voted worst-dressed guy on the block. My figure was perfect for a uniform and I knew it. God, I wanted that uniform.

The world was at war and every night I sat by a friend's radio and listened to the events. I'd heard about the courage of the pilots in the Army Air Corps. In the morning they

---

*Her act of generosity has never been forgotten. When I became a coach a few years later, I decided to buy a letter jacket for at least one athlete who couldn't afford it. Sometimes I bought more. Mrs. McDonald started a tradition. Now the first black captain in the Florence police force, Spencer Butler, does the same thing. In 1990, I went to visit Mrs. McDonald. I showed her the sweater she gave me in 1942. It was an emotional reunion with tears filling her eyes as well as mine.

were front-page news. I couldn't wait to fly the airborne version of a boxcar. For all I knew I'd find my dad in the back chewing on a straw. I could see myself dropping bombs, talking trash, and strutting my stuff in Piccadilly.

I didn't make the cut. I was too young and didn't have enough schooling. I was disappointed until I heard there was a special unit being formed called the Air Commandos. I volunteered. They sent me to Lakeland Air Force Base to be trained. It was tough. Guys were dropping out and everyone was complaining about the heat. I knew they had never been in a cotton field.

A few months later we were ready to go. I was in the first group that was headed to Asia. A few days before we were to leave someone realized our contingent was too large for the assigned aircraft. Three needed to be cut. They went alphabetically. Weaver, Williams, and Yoast would be reassigned to the second attack group. I was upset because I wanted to mix it up. A short while later, group number one launched and was destroyed over Burma. The casualties were appalling. When President Truman got the news he put an end to the program. My commando days were over.

While I was hanging around waiting for them to figure out what to do with me, I saw a poster for a fitness contest. I entered and set the Army record for sit-ups: 1700. I would have done 1701 but I had worn the skin off my lower back and decided to stop. A commanding officer witnessed my effort and reasoned I should become a physical training instructor. That was fine by me. My brain may not develop but my biceps would.

I was shipped to Georgia to do my thing. Initially, I was

a little intimidated. I don't know if it was because my ears were still damp or the fact that it was the first time I'd been put in charge of anyone. I got over it. I knew how tough the enemy was. I knew my job was to make my guys even tougher. I accepted the challenge.

What I noticed was that not only did my students get stronger but so did I. Responsibility has a way of putting hair on your chest. One day I looked in the mirror. I liked what I saw.

A week later I was at the Dilly Twirl having a cone and showing my triceps. A beauty sitting at a nearby table seemed to being paying attention so I gave her a smile. She tossed one back. It wasn't just any smile. That smile told me she liked the wiggle in my walk. I asked her name. She said Blanche.

Physically, I was a man but emotionally I was somewhere else. At that moment in time, the only date I'd ever had came in a jar from Spain. My coach in high school didn't help. Coach Braly told me girls and sports went together like a pepper and a malt. I stayed away.

Now I knew better. I wanted a date. I'd have died for a date.

SHORT STORY SHORTER

We fell in love and got married. Blanche's dad was a caretaker for the Whitney Plantation in Thomasville. We had full run of the place. On a number of occasions I came around the bend to find General Eisenhower and Admiral Halsey shooting quail and chewing the fat. One day Ike and

Bull looked at me. A few days later I was shipped to the Lone Star state. I know it was a coincidence.

Blanche came along. She got pregnant. I was sent away. She got lonely. I was still away. She delivered Susan Gail. I was far away. She said, "you're not for me." I said I understood.

I would have been more hurt but the waters did not run that deep. We never really had time to get to know each other. There was too much going on. Love blooms through experiences, good and bad, and with Blanche I had few.

Years went by. The war ended. I'd done what they asked me to do. I thought I did it well but there was no reason to put my picture on a Wheaties box. In 1946 I was told I could go home. It takes a short time in the military to understand you only do what people tell you. I wasn't going to make a move without permission. I called D.C. and asked if I could go somewhere else. "Whatever," came the reply. I enrolled in the Georgia Military College. It was a turning point in my life. I met people who were kind and thoughtful and smart. I saw them make a difference in other people's lives. I knew they had in mine. An image appeared. It was a long dusty road filled with bumps but at the end I could see a sheepskin. I would become a teacher. That meant Mercer University.

I enrolled and shifted into overdrive. I had one ambition: to be the best teacher I could become. I met a guy by the name of Ed Sanders. We shared a common vision. We both wanted to accomplish something. Ed was my kind of guy. He was a tenacious personality and by hanging with him I adopted some of his traits. One day I ran into him and he was all excited. He was so proud that he'd been hired to be a lifeguard. I was happy for Ed but concerned for whoever might need his help. Ed didn't swim. I figured he'd find a way.

We studied hard, played basketball, and ran track. Every now and then we had a Dr. Pepper. We joined the Sigma Nu fraternity. Ed told me getting a paddle broke over my butt would be fun. He lied. I didn't hold it against him. Ed is still my friend. Why not? I learned friendship and furniture are much alike. If you invest in quality it won't have to be replaced.

I worked hard at Mercer University and I could feel my brain getting stronger. It felt awfully good. One day they gave me a diploma. The next day I was standing on the corner eating some peanuts wondering what to do. A Greyhound pulled up with a sign that said it was going east. I got on board. When the doors opened, I stepped out in Sparta, Georgia.

I looked around. It looked okay. I had a nickel in my pocket but I wasn't worried. I knew my million-dollar attitude would see me through. I've always been an optimist. I think much of it had to do with my mom. She told me over and over, "Son, we may not have much but there are people who have less." I knew she was right. I'd seen the one room shack filled with ten and a Thanksgiving turkey that looked like a mouse. Those words have always been with me.

I landed a job as teacher. My gosh. I was about to trade overalls for a white shirt and tie. My mom was proud. My dad didn't know.

It was time to get to work. I dove into my responsibilities as a teacher and coach. I loved working with kids and there was a lot of work to be done. On one side of the tracks, Mint Juleps bloomed and on the other side desperation. In Sparta, in 1950 if you didn't look like a cream puff you got the short end of the stick, if you got any stick at all. For some reason it made me mad. I'm not sure why because I'd had a checkered history with racism. I followed the rules. I drank from the white man's fountain and sat in the front of the bus.

In looking back on it I think most of the kids I grew up with had a contaminated view of equality. If your skin was black you were a "nigger." When I was young and dumb I didn't pay much attention. Poverty was on my mind. As my brain got more wrinkles, I felt a lot different. I came to hate that word. For what it meant and for what it did.

All my life I had known black people and I couldn't remember one that had done me wrong. As a matter of fact, had it not been for Aunt Mary and some of her cousins I might still be in that field.

The more I saw the madder I got. I started speaking up. I found myself losing friends. I found myself making friends. For every bigot that said goodbye, someone else said hello. I was a church-going guy and somewhere I'd heard, *Seek Only the Respect of Those You Respect.* If Mary thought I was okay, I'd be fine.

A while later I fell in love again. Her name was Dorothy Beall. We got married. Dot wanted a child. She got pregnant and I was overjoyed. This daughter I would raise. No one would take her from me. I was right. But what I didn't know was that God had a plan. He took her mom. Dorothy died on the delivery table.

I can remember holding Bonnie Jean in my arms, looking in her eyes and loving who looked back. I knew it would
be tough raising her by myself but I was ready. Shortly after
the funeral Dot's parents approached me. They didn't think
I could do their granddaughter right. They said they'd made
arrangements to take her. I said no.

I placated the pain with hard work and getting Bonnie
Jean walking. I continued to teach and coach. I wasn't happy
with the racial climate but I had enough to keep me busy so
I plowed ahead. I could feel my anger growing. It soon
turned to gloom.

A black baseball team had a game in the park where the
class D teams played. The ball field was near the school gym.
The showers in their bathhouse didn't work. The solution
was simple. I talked with their coach and told him they could
use the showers in the high school. He was hesitant. I guess
he knew a whole lot more about racism than I did. He understood the implication of that act. I didn't. I convinced
him it wasn't a problem. He told me they didn't need to
shower. I now realize he was probably trying to protect me.
I took a stand and they got clean. As they walked out of the
locker room each ball player made a point of shaking my
hand and thanking me. I was surprised because I thought it
was no big deal. I was wrong.

Next morning, the chairman of the school board was
knocking on my door and she was mad. "Come with me,"
she commanded. I obeyed. We went to the store and bought
soap, detergent, and disinfectant. We went back and
scrubbed the showers. For an hour I got to listen to her tirade. It was personal. Her son played on the high school

team and the last thing he was going to do was shower where a nigger had used the soap.

The next day I was counseled about being color-blind. I decided it was time to leave. I could hear Roswell, Georgia calling my name. I took my daughter and headed out. It was 1954 and I was back at work. I coached football and track. I raised my girl and enrolled in a master's program.

Experience had taught me good and bad fortune usually arrives unexpectedly. That sure was the case. One day I was working in the student center, when the most beautiful girl in the world walked up and asked me a question. Her name was Betty Watson. Looking at her my heart began to thump. My tongue got tied. I was having trouble getting the words out. She gave me a pass.

I'd seen Betty around and on a few occasions heard her talking about sports. I figured that was my ace in the hole. Roger Bannister had just broken the four-minute mile so I played that card. She responded enthusiastically. I asked her some other stuff. She had answers. It turned out she was an athlete. Her life centered on sports and games. In ping-pong when Betty was my opponent I got killed. She could fish. I'd bring in a minnow and she would hook a whale. There was nothing she couldn't play and nothing she couldn't do.

I'd never met a woman like Betty. In the south, at that time, if you wore a dress, sweat was a sin. I couldn't believe my good fortune. She was beautiful, smart, funny, generous, and best of all she had pants and sneakers too. We started thinking about a future. She told her parents she'd met a guy. They were overjoyed. She explained I had a child. They were underwhelmed. I could understand it. Like any parent

17

they wanted the best for their daughter. Becoming a wife and mother on the same day could be tough. Maybe for someone else but not for Betty. She had the biggest heart I'd ever seen.

She said she'd be my wife. The next day we went to the courthouse and tied the knot. The date was July 11, 1955. Her parents weren't happy. It wasn't that they didn't like me it was just that they could see trouble ahead. They were right.

We went back to Roswell. I had my hands full coaching everything in sight. One day she told me she would take the girl's basketball team off my hands. I let her have it. They got better. I can tell you a thousand things that made Betty special or I can tell you one. She was the most enthusiastic person I'd ever met. And it was that enthusiasm that made others excited.

We were a team. Betty was my wife, lover, confidante, and best friend. I didn't know how I had gotten to that point without her. One day she came home with a smile on her face. She said she was hungry. I asked what she wanted. She replied, "A pickle and a shake. Put a little Tabasco on top." Nine months later she delivered Angela. The date was August 19, 1956.

An opportunity opened up south of the Mason-Dixon Line. Betty and I talked about it and decided it was time to go. In 1960, we moved to Alexandria, Virginia. It was a major step for us. It was a different world. Being next to Washington, D.C., we thought we were in the center of the universe. It was nice that they didn't roll up the streets at noon but there was a cost associated with that. Alexandria was much more expensive and we had a hard time making ends meet. But in her typical Betty Watson fashion she kept all the balls in the air while I worked on my career.

I had a job at Hammond High School teaching and coaching. Hammond sat in the most prestigious part of Alexandria and if the kids I coached didn't have silver spoons in their mouths it was because they were getting dry-cleaned. Initially I coached track and the junior varsity football team. I was having success doing both. We were raising our two daughters and things were moving on.

Betty got pregnant again. A lot of things have been said about me over the years; good and bad but nobody has ever said Bill Yoast couldn't make kids. Sheryl arrived February 5, 1962.

BLACK CLOUDS ON THE HORIZON

It was 1964 and my football team had just gone undefeated. I decided to go home early one afternoon and celebrate with Betty. When I arrived she wasn't there but I could hear some loud music coming from Bonnie Jean's room. I was surprised because she should have been at school. I knocked on the door and walked in. On the table, a container filled with incense was burning to the beat of a Hari Krishna drum. I didn't give it much thought. I asked her why she was home and she told me she was sick. I gave her the benefit of the doubt. Given that she was acting like her distracted teenage self I decided I'd leave her alone and go celebrate the season with a glass of milk and some cookies. In retrospect it was a terrible decision.

THE WAKE-UP CALL

I don't know anybody who has ever achieved anything that didn't question what they were doing. It's what makes responsible people responsible. Self-assessment provides a compass that can keep you outta the swamp. In 1966, I found myself in the middle of the Okefenokee. Surprising in that my football teams a couple years earlier had run a string to 20-0.

The '66 season that was to be . . . never was. The ticker tape parade took place on foreign soil. I was up to my neck in crocodiles and all of them knew my name.

It was during this period I started to have marital problems. I knew I was working too late. My nerves were frayed. I talked with an edge. Stress had stolen my smile. One day the papers arrived. Betty wanted a divorce. I was despondent. I thought we could work it out but I didn't know the depth of the problem. A while later we showed up in front of the judge. His frown could sour sugar. He read the decree. As he looked at my wife you could see the sympathy in his eyes. He looked at me with a scowl.

"I'm in agreement with Betty, Bill. Any coach who can't win "The Big One" doesn't deserve a wife." I looked at Betty and asked her to give me one more chance. Her smile told me she would.

I wanted to blame someone else. I thought fate had done me wrong. And then one day I looked in the mirror. It didn't help. A mirror only reflects what's on the outside. I knew to fix the situation I had to get at the core of who I was. Failure may not be fatal but it sure hurts. I wanted the pain to go away. I figured there were two things I could do—placate my ego with excuses or fix the problem. I took the less painful route.

I have to confess. I was surprised by my approach. I decided to open my mind. Math teachers are known for precision. Science centers on being exact. There is no maybe in two plus two. Coaching is a different issue. Alternatives abound. Could it be what made me a digital wizard hindered me as a coach?

I pulled out a pad and began my search for the Holy Grail. I began to write down everything that came to mind. Nothing was off limits. At the top I had headings. Coach, Leader, Teacher, Parent, Priest. On the side I had Actions. In the middle, Reactions. I had arrows and numbers. Within minutes the page was filled. On to page two. More scribbling. More notes. Successes. Failures. Examples. Role Models. Input. Output. My mind raced. On to page three. Two days later I'd filled the pad. I went to the fridge and grabbed a Coke. I lit a fire and sat down. I wasn't getting up until I figured out what went wrong.

A NEW BEGINNING

As I looked at the chicken scratch and tried to find meaning amidst the mess, I went into a state of shock. I couldn't believe it. The words jumped off the page. No, it can't be true. Yes it is, I concluded. I'm not as dumb as I thought. And then I remembered. I didn't get the job because I'd been a loser. I scrutinized my past. It looked pretty good. Two years earlier the Mayor asked to bronze my whistle. Miss Alexandria wanted to drink Gatorade from my cleats. I was feeling better.

I gazed at the words and found meaning everywhere. Sure, fate had not been kind, but I'd also made mistakes. The good news was they could be fixed. With some modifications and a little luck, Yoast would be back. Glory Hallelujah.

THE BIRTH OF A PLAN

If you didn't know it, your responsibility as a coach, or parent, or priest, or teacher is no different than any leader. Intuitively, I've always known that leadership played a role in achievement. The luckiest kids are those that get to grow up under leadership. From the very beginning they are directed, counseled, nurtured, and guided by someone who cares. They're encouraged to extend themselves. They are put in situations where there is an upside and downside and asked to perform. They're challenged to excel. More often than not they do. As a result, confidence grows. And the confidence that comes from testing yourself and winning manifests itself in a variety of ways—none more important than the creation of energy. People that are well led are filled with energy. They are excited, enthusiastic, and optimistic. Children that are blessed by leadership know that anything is attainable.

As young men and women came into my life I could tell almost instantly which ones had a leader in their life and which ones didn't. Kids that had been well led were up for anything. All I had to do was make a suggestion and they were after it.

On the other side of the coin, kids who had grown up without leadership were less open, less adaptive, and more hesitant. Coaching them is where I earned my pay. Making them better was when I felt the best.

Leadership at times can be overwhelming. There are many who think about leadership and see icons. They visualize countries on the march and armadas preparing to do battle. Some believe there isn't anything small about leadership. I think they're wrong.

Leadership has nothing to do with size or scope. Believe it or not most results start at the bottom and work their way up. The performance of a thousand little groups determines the performance of the parent. World War II was won with a lot of little teams shooting rifles. Great companies are made on the assembly line and in customer service. Forget to put the screw in the widget and it will be felt across the country. Five people answering the phone correctly are how reputations are built.

Most of the championships I've won did not come from anything notable. An undetected effort in the middle of the line sprung a running back free. One effort by one player made the difference and the rest was history.

So if you are thinking you have to come up with something profound think again. Think small and if things aren't working out, think even smaller.

Little stuff counts.

There is a common thread that runs through every leadership action. All leaders have a goal and that is to produce results. Leadership involves doing something. Leadership involves accomplishing something.

Leaders are called many things and you can add catalyst to the list. Leaders are a catalyst for generating emotion because emotion is at the heart of elevating performance. Your MO as a leader may require that you be smart, aggressive, creative, humble, clever, disciplined, courageous, empathetic, or invisible. In a leader's bag of tricks there are numerous tools to get people excited. Excitement creates energy and energy creates results.

NO STEROIDS NEEDED

One year while coaching track I had to place two runners in the top four to win the state meet. One of them, David Sullivan, had never run the 440. I knew he was a competitor. I went and told him I thought he could beat my ace 440 man, Jasper Kirk. He liked the sound of that. I went to my 440 guy and told him I couldn't believe what I just heard.

"What's that's coach?" he asked. "David just told me he could beat you in the 440 and he doesn't even run the 440." I could see the fire in his eyes. "Bring him on coach," he replied. They finished one and two and we took the title. Who won? The team.

When people are well led they do amazing things. They do incredible things. They do unexplainable things. They will give their life for their leader and have no regrets. Examples abound.

If you are going to get your team to a higher level of accomplishment don't hesitate to ask for more. Don't be afraid to demand more. That's your job. I've never met anyone who didn't want to do better. I've never met anyone who didn't appreciate the person who made them a success. Since the beginning people have responded to leadership but there are some things about leadership that the non-leader doesn't understand.

- People liked to be led.
- They will decide who they will follow.
- Their effort sprouts from emotion.

In its simplest form, leadership is about looking out for someone else. The people that are following you aren't dumb. They know, through your actions, whether their welfare is at the forefront of your thoughts. You can't fake it. And when your followers determine you are doing right by them, they will do right by you. With leadership, dreams are fulfilled.

In 1966, none were. There were lots of reasons. The

non-leader in me would like to point a finger but the leader in me accepts responsibility. It was my job to get it done and I didn't. My guys wanted a championship. I gave them a black eye. As their leader I failed. End of story.

I've spent a great deal of time thinking about leadership. I believe it is at the heart of performance. I didn't always know that. When I first began coaching I read all the books, I memorized techniques, I focused on strategy. Tactics were my thing. My X-ing and O-ing was as good as it gets.

What I didn't understand initially was that all of that meant nothing if I couldn't get my players to elevate their effort.

I used to think leading was easy. I've changed my mind. If leading was easy we wouldn't have political unrest, business debacles, and armed insurrection. If leading was easy, insolence would be passé, bad guys would be good and good guys would be better. If leading were easy I'd still have a wife.

Leading is not easy. Taking a group to a higher level has never been easy. Understanding how it happens is very easy. We all know that leadership has changed the world. I've never seen any situation in any environment that wasn't made better with leadership and worse without it. Over the years I've wondered why people don't lead. Given the link between leadership and success and non-leadership and failure, why wouldn't anyone in a leadership position lead? I've come to the conclusion that there are a variety of factors— fear of failure, ignorance, apathy, and the burden that accompanies fulfilling expectation. Being asked to make a team victorious can be daunting.

People that follow you want to win. Victory has a nice ring. Thinking you may not be able to give it to them could make you hesitate. I read a quote once that I've never forgotten.

On the plains of hesitation lie the bones of countless millions, who at the dawn of victory chose to wait and in their waiting, died.

I'd like to give credit to whoever said that but I don't know the name. I'd like to thank him because the words are accurate.

In leading others, action is what matters. Action is the catalyst. Thinking about something is fine. Talking about it is nice. But only through action will one of two things happen. You will fail or you will succeed. Either way, you win. Failure will make you smarter. Success will make you stronger. So when you act, there is always a benefit. It may not be immediate but then life is not three innings.

Over the years, I've encountered people who are slaves to the "what if" game. I believe those are the two laziest words around. If you are asking yourself, "what if" then it means you haven't done anything.

If you have done something you will have your answer. You will know that what you did was right or wrong. I had great expectations for the 1966 Hammond season. Sure the talent on our squad had been cut in half but we still had the core of a team that went undefeated. In all the key positions I had guys who had performed. There was one guy I was a little worried about. He was my quarterback and a linebacker. I guess that said something about his personality. It wasn't that he couldn't play he just had an opinion about everything. He was the personification of the mouth that roared. Good for calling plays but no coach wants to be scolded by an eighteen year old.

It seemed every five minutes he was critiquing my bread and butter. "Come on coach," he'd yell, "enough of this running stuff. Let's put the ball in the air." Periodically I'd let him elevate. The results were always the same. At sixty yards he would put a bullet on a receiver's numbers. At forty yards he could knock 'em down. I was in agreement with my coaching staff that he had an arm but disagreed with them that we should employ it.

For a number of years my offense had served me well. It would again. I'd never been a passing coach. That was a different game. Throwing on first and ten was uncharted water and I didn't want to go on the rocks. So I was afraid, afraid to change.

Because I believe that a willingness to change is so crucial to success, it demands comment.

Change: Doing what needs to be done under different circumstances.

In the course of getting down the road I never gave change much consideration. It was probably because I was too busy changing. I thought a lot about kids. I thought a lot about coaching. I never thought much about change. And I don't know why, because my life has been a never-ending series of changes. At the age of thirty-six I had changed so much I sometimes wondered who I was. In the decade following my graduating from college I was on the move. I'm still on the move. I'm ready to reinvent myself again. At this stage I don't know what that will be but I'm excited by the thought that in the not too distant future I know my life will become different. How? It doesn't matter.

And so the first thing I would point out is that:

♦ Change is inevitable.

It is so understood that statement is a cliché. Whether it is by choice or by edict you will have to change in your life. Maybe you've never given change much thought. You might not realize how much change you've experienced. I suspect you've changed more than you realize. And more change is coming. Accept it because it is change that will deliver the unforeseen thrill.

You should also know that:

♦ Change comes unexpectedly.

There are those who believe change is essential and they are prepared to give it a kiss. What I've found though is that many of these people believe change arrives on the horizon riding a white horse and wearing a ten-gallon hat. You can't miss it. Emblazoned across its chest are the letters C-H-A-N-G-E. It's on its way. You have time to prepare. In reality, you open a door or turn a corner and there it is. "Hi," it says. "Here we go." And if you aren't ready you may say no.

♦ Change is disruptive.

It's supposed to be. If it weren't, it wouldn't be change. Change is about mixing things up. Whether it is troublesome is up to you. Recognize that in the disruption lies alternatives and solutions that will take you places you didn't know existed.

Change is so necessary, so important, so life sustaining I've often wondered why so many people resist it. I've come to the conclusion that there are three reasons. Do they look familiar?

Apathy. Some people have been disengaged for so long their mind, their body, their spirit has atrophied. When the need for change comes they just aren't interested.

Ignorance. People who don't understand what to do usually do nothing.

Fear. Change is notorious for taking us out of our comfort zone. It interrupts our life. It forces us to be different. It mandates we operate with a new set of rules. That can be frightening. I don't know too many people who don't hesitate when they encounter something that scares them. But the difference between people who accomplish more and those that accomplish less lies in the recognition that fear is never rewarded. Overcoming it is.

Skiing is a great metaphor for life. Standing at the top of a double black diamond looking down a run filled with ice-encrusted moguls, you wonder what to do. The inclination is to sit back, go slow, and survive the event. The reality is, hesitation is seldom rewarded. In skiing, the answer to fear is force. The same thing applies to change. When change occurs you need to attack. Easier said than done. For people who have had little change, change is a big deal. I won't tell you that it shouldn't make you uncomfortable. It will. To this day change always grabs my gut but then when I think about what change has done for me, I'm ready to do it again.

Seventy percent of coaching is getting players properly placed where they can be most effective. I tried to avoid preconceived notions. A difficult thing. On the Titans we had a young man who was in full bloom at seventeen. At 6'5", 240 lbs he was a moose. We thought we had the next Bubba Smith. We put him at defensive end. In a scrimmage with the Girl Scouts he got buried. What a surprise. We played another game and he got killed. I put him on the bench. A few weeks later I got a brainstorm. I decided to give him a try at tackle. The difference between a two or three point stance made all the difference. Why? It doesn't matter. What is important is that the operative word that led to victory was change. He went on to become an All-American and one of the most recruited guys in the country.

In the course of getting to this point, my attitudes about things have undergone a number of changes. To this day I find myself evolving in all aspects of my life. Maybe Darwin had it correct. The survival of the species is predicated on its ability to adapt. Surprisingly I've become more flexible with age.

In part, my evolution started after reading a story by Arthur Conan Doyle. The title was *A Study in Scarlet*.

The main character, as you probably know, is Sherlock Holmes.

Let me paraphrase what happened. Dr. Watson, Sherlock Holmes's assistant, was interested in why Sherlock had such a profound knowledge in matters related to crime but when it came to knowing things unrelated to crime, he was in the dark—a first-class dummy. Watson was confused. One day Holmes explained it to him. "I see my brain as an attic. I can store whatever I want. If I store too many things, when I go to look for something that is important, it will be more difficult to find."

It made sense. At that point in my coaching career maybe I had too much in my attic. I'd read all the books. I had the facts. At least I thought I did. At the time I didn't know that a lot of experts have a self-serving interest in their sermon. Maybe the real good stuff was not so good after all. For me, victories were becoming as hard to grasp as a feather on a windy day. So I examined the hypothesis. Were there things in my cerebral storage shed that were obstacles to progress? I concluded yes.

FAST FORWARD

The next season, 1967, was greeted with hope and also a little skepticism. I was still recovering from the emotional shock of a losing season but my success in coaching track had helped rebuild my ego.

I didn't have the hot shots from the previous year. This group was pretty much a team of untested unknowns. There was something about them though that made me feel good. My quarterback had graduated and my earplugs had been retired. The new guy that was going to spearhead the offense was a plump, unassuming sophomore named John O'Connor. He was a perfect example of the book and cover concept. Looking at him you suspected he was the most valuable player at Pizza Hut. John O'Connor wasn't a cover boy but as an athletic talent he was terrific. And he could think. And he could throw. And he could kick. And he was quiet. Thank God he was quiet.

I started, with the help of my coaches, to evaluate my players. It didn't take long to recognize that not only did I have a guy who could put the football down field but Bob Stumpf could catch it.

It was time to change. Opportunity was knocking. I opened the door and attacked. The air was filled with pigskin. The turnaround had begun. Our fans returned to the stands. On Friday night no one was watching ice dancing. The gridiron was back in vogue. A year later we won the Championship. Mistakenly, I got Coach of the Year.

The good times were punctuated on August 27, 1968, when my daughter Deidre was born. Not only was she a great kid but she also turned out to be a great athlete.

In those two years I redefined who I was—as coach, as a leader, as a human being. I learned that commitment transcended desire. Commitment had to be directed. Being committed in the wrong areas would do nothing. Commitment was not a salve or a tattoo. Commitment did not vanish with circumstance. Commitment was a force that resided within. Commitment dictated results. Commitment was at the core of excellence.

I also learned that loyalty sprouted from integrity and integrity is at the heart of a coach/player relationship. I learned so many things and I would need them all.

NAVIGATING THE MAZE

If you're like me, you've spent some time thinking about who you are and why you're here. I'll bet you even wonder where you're going. I still do. And even though I've given my journey considerable thought, I continue to struggle with what it all means. Figuring this stuff out can make your head hurt.

Somewhere back when, I was investigating the meaning of Yoast. I knew I wanted to achieve something but wasn't sure what that meant. Big house, fast car, fifty dollar bills. I'd been persuaded that if I didn't have a pinky ring, I was a nobody. One day I borrowed a friend's. I didn't feel any better.

Shortly thereafter I was reading a book about Albert Schweitzer. The story chronicled the journey of a man who abandoned the "good life" for the good of others. There was this quote:

I do not know what your destiny will be but I do know this. The only ones among you who will be truly happy are those that have sought and found how to serve.

Something inside me came alive. Now all I had to do was figure out where to begin. As I gave it some thought I was cascaded with options. I wanted to serve but didn't know how. I didn't know who. I didn't know where. What seemed so simple became complex. I turned to a friend for help.

She suggested a book of philosophy. Actually it was a book of philosophers. They were all there: Spinoza, Socrates, Bacon, Voltaire. The only one missing was Mr. Rogers. I was teleported to different worlds. Plato said justice involves a balance between give and take. Machiavelli told me to take all that I could get. Aristotle suggested I let the smart guys call the plays. My brain burned as I tried to interpret how it applied it to me.

Somewhere in the fog I was presented with the story of the Gordian knot. According to Greek legend a peasant named Gordius arrived in the square of Phrygia in an ox cart. A few years earlier an oracle had foretold that the future King would come to town riding in a wagon. Seeing Gordius, the populace gave him the throne. In gratitude, Gordius dedicated the wagon to Zeus and tied it up using a very intricate knot—the Gordian knot. It was so complex no one could untie it. Many tried. Theories abounded: pull it, push it, spank it, kick it. Some used oil and others tried spit. Untying the knot resisted all. Another oracle predicted whomever solved the puzzle would become the Lord of Asia.

Failure ensued until the year 333 B.C. when Alexander the Great came upon it. He took a look. He wanted clarification. He asked a question. Did Gordius say the knot had to be untied or undone? His interpretation determined his course of action. He pulled out his sword and the knot was freed. A light went on. Thanks to a sword-and-sandals guy I figured out, in life, there were options.

Over the years I've been asked to explain my coaching philosophy. I used to think why would anyone care what I thought. I'm a country boy. Philosophy is for others. If you want philosophy go to Greece. Then one day, someone pointed out to me that experience is like a sponge. If you go down enough paths a bucket of stuff gets absorbed. If you don't use the lessons it's trash but if you do, it's philosophy. If that's the criterion then maybe I do have a philosophy.

A number of years ago I was watching an interview with one of the most successful writers of all time. He had written a book that had helped millions of people examine their life and find a better way. He was a bona-fide All-American "Thinkmeister."

The interviewer asked him why we were here. My ears came alert. I always wondered why they planted me in Alabama. I got goose bumps thinking about what he would say. I myself had pondered that question on more than one occasion. The cotton field gave me Mary. The student center delivered Betty. But why was I here? I sat up in my seat. I wanted the skinny.

He hesitated, looked up at the heavens, took a deep breath and proclaimed, "We are here to learn." The interviewer collapsed with joy, that such profundity had been uttered on his show. I took it in and initially thought he was right on the mark. About ten seconds later I started to question the statement. Learning is great because without learning there is no knowledge. But if all we are doing is improving our own situation then isn't that a self-centered exercise? Is that why we are here? Is life about me? I don't think so.

He was right on when he said learning was important but he was one rung short on the ladder to fulfillment. We learn so that we can make a contribution. When a person contributes, others benefit.

A while later, I was told a story about that author. He was still delivering thoughts on how to get through life but his own life was in shambles. I wasn't surprised.

Recently I was asked by an interviewer to discuss my philosophy. Sometimes I use my words but every now and then I go back to that cotton field and channel what Mary said. She wanted to contribute and her philosophy is never out of reach. I delivered my sermon.

I looked in the interviewer's eyes. There was no reaction. I knew why. Giving a pearl to a pig was a waste of a pearl. I didn't take it personally. I'd been rejected before. I thought about explaining why those ideals were important. But I realized it would be futile. I knew he didn't care. I knew he would not embrace something he did not value. For him, they were just words spewing from an old man.

In the course of living my life I have learned the hard way that there are lots of people that don't care. Early on I spent too much time trying to get them in the groove. At some point I realized my effort could be better spent elsewhere.

Caring and character are inextricably linked and it is character that provides the foundation on which a country, a family or a team can be built. Some people are born with character, but more often than not, character is developed by overcoming adversity. And that happens with behaviors that I call Performance Drivers. They look like words: Integrity, Commitment, Determination, Courage, and Enthusiasm. In reality, they are the building blocks of excellence.

There was a time in my life when I was swayed by appearance. Way back when, someone once asked me what I looked for in a quarterback. My reply, "square jaw, thick hair, good teeth." I hadn't learned yet that character was invisible.

Tracye Funn was blessed with character. She was a high jumper and hurdler on the T.C. Williams track team and I was her coach. Some people need encouragement to raise the performance bar but Tracye wasn't one of them. She was always challenging herself. "Get it up coach," she'd shout. Initially, the result was always the same. She didn't clear the bar and more often than not it resulted in a bump or bruise. Her legs were covered with scrapes. She understood they were the price of success.

Years later she took that same attitude into the business world. Raising the hurdle might be painful but it was the only way to succeed. She did. She became the first black president of the Prince Georges County Chamber of Commerce. I was the speaker at her inauguration. At the end I asked her to lift up her dress and show the scars on her legs. She respectfully declined citing that hurdle was a little too low.

Character is important and it blossoms when easy turns hard. If you want your team to have character make it difficult on them. If you want your kids to have character ensure the "rite of passage" is tougher than a day at Disney World. Everywhere you look the people that we respect, we admire, we honor . . . have character.

I was sitting with a friend shortly after a number of Wall Street scandals erupted. The subject of character came up. We discussed it in detail. We agreed that character was at the heart of the problem. If you looked at the track records of the most egregious you would see that they had lived a pretty cushy life. Had they experienced how tough it was to earn a shiny dollar they might have given it more respect. Had they spent some time in a cotton field with Mary, we'd all be better off.

I can't remember anyone I've known that had it tough and wasn't grateful for the experience. They overcame hardship and were proud of it. It's character that turns bad into better.

If you're looking to build a dynasty of excellence start with people who have a few nooks and crannies. It's not all that hard to spot. When someone walks through your door and tells you they got kicked in the head, punched in the face, and pistol-whipped while trying to get milk money for mom, smile, because you may have just discovered a Titan.

I can tell you, in the course of getting to where you want to go, there are going to be some potholes en route. As a matter of fact, something dark lies just beyond the horizon and it's waiting for you. The good news is character is waiting for it. When sweet times turn sour and happy turns sad, when the ill wind blows with hurricane force, if you've surrounded yourself with character you're going to make it.

I've had teams that were big and fast and lost. I've had teams that were small and slow and won. What made the difference? I can tell you it was intangible.

Life has a way of telling you when you are on the road to nowhere. Look for signs. Starting out can be pretty scary. If you are smart enough, one morning you wake up and scream. You just realized your mom and dad are going to sell your bed. When that happens you'd better be able to answer the call. Figuring out the deal can be the difference between having a meal or becoming one. It has always been a tough world and it is going to get tougher. The good news is that if you have prepared yourself properly your success is guaranteed. That's right. The people at the top didn't get there by accident. They knew what to do and they did it. There wasn't much wishing and hoping.

I've always believed that the foundation to accomplishment started with knowledge. I wanted players that were smart. There was a time when I thought information was the key. It was all about facts, facts, and more facts. Later on I learned that information without experience is like a wheel without spokes, a sail without wind, a person without direction, a soul without values.

Experience is a great teacher. I've found nothing better than experience to teach the lessons I wanted learned.

Someone once told me a story about a very successful old man. He was getting an award for achievement. A young man approached him and asked how he had accomplished so much. He replied two words: good decisions. The young man asked how do you make good decisions? The man answered one word: experience. The young man inquired as to how to get experience. The old man answered. Two words: bad decisions.

I've made a lot of bad decisions but I've learned from every one of them. I've seldom been embarrassed twice. I guess I must have understood if I didn't fix what was broken someone was going to sell my bed. Too many people get stuck in a rut. And if you stay in one long enough it can become a grave. Whether you are coaching a team, raising a family, or holding down an emperorship, stay nimble. Things will never stop changing, and if you don't flow with the current you can get obsolete fast. The only way to find out if the snake oil works is to give it a try.

A TITANIC EVENT

Dreams come in stages. If you've done things right, your confidence grows and your aspirations too. In the world of large dreams though, mine were pretty small. I never thought about being President, Allied Commander, or CEO. I did once dream about eight seconds on a bull. No way.

At one point in my life, my dream was to fill my belly. Thirty years later it was to fill a stadium.

The rumors had been circulating for a while. Hammond High was going down. And George Washington was too. A few years earlier a superschool had been built and its time had come. It just made economic sense. If the plan went according to Hoyle, T.C. Williams would have more kids than Peru. That was an opportunity and a problem—a problem because at that moment in time, race relations had taken a dramatic turn south. All over America the flames of racial hatred burned. And they had made their way to 3330 King Street. In theory, the objective was noble but in reality when you compress that many kids into that small an area you're going to have problems. Combining a predominantly black high school, GW, with its predominantly white arch-rival didn't help. And when trouble arrived it came with a vengeance.

I would have been more concerned but I had been dealing with racial issues all my life. I'd gotten pretty skilled at getting people together. I was ready. One morning the phone rang. "Bill," the caller said. "It's yours." I was thrilled. Another dream had been realized.

Shortly thereafter a number of catastrophic racial events took place. Some were local and others were far away. It didn't matter. When you have too many cooks, cooking a plan, things can happen. A few days later I got another call. The voice was a friend. He hemmed and hawed, took me in circles and then apologized and then took me in some more circles and then apologized again. I asked, "Do you have something to tell me?" "Bill," the caller said "you've been replaced by another." Already? I thought. The season hadn't started. Practice was a week away. I was 0 for 0 and getting the boot. "It's only temporary," he added. "Don't worry Bill, you'll get it back." At the time I didn't know what that meant. I asked who the new coach was. He told me. "He's the guy from North Carolina. He's got a good record. He's also black, Bill, and that might be helpful for the situation."

Black, white, pink, or green I didn't give a hoot. All I knew was a guy named H-E-R-M-A-N was taking my job.

A few years later, a reporter asked me how it felt to have

the brass ring in my hand and then have it taken away. I thought about the question. I decided I would use a fishing analogy. "It's like pulling in a fifty pound salmon after a two-hour fight. You get it to the bank. You picture it on the grill and taste it in your mouth. All of a sudden . . . it's gone." His face remained blank. So I continued, "as you stumble back to camp, you get mugged, tarred and feathered, tied to a cactus, and flogged." I detected a tear in his eye. He was feeling my pain. I went for the dunk. "And then I got to go home and tell my daughters their Head Coach Dad had been demoted from a tuba to a second fiddle.

Did that decision by the school board hurt? You bet. And disappointment that great can make you want to blame. I thought I had the right. Over the next few weeks I watched the images of the hatred that was tearing America apart. At some point it dawned on me. Bill Yoast was a minnow in a big sea. What I wanted was irrelevant. It didn't matter. On the world stage far greater people had been treated worse. Maybe the board was right. The answer to our city's problem was a guy named Boone.

I had a number of perceptions about the man who was going to replace me. Most of it came from the grapevine. Detractors said one thing and supporters said another. The air was filled with lies. I heard Herman got results with a gun. They said he was mean and nasty. Wore spurs. Carried a blade. It got worse. They said his teeth were false.

His fans said something else. He came to earth on a lightning bolt. He was a master motivator—disciplined, determined, smart, and cool. His shoes had wings. Some said he taught Zeus how to punt and Louis Armstrong which end of the trumpet to stick in his mouth. The word was that HB was a Renaissance man. They said Herman had the plan.

This went on for weeks. One day a headline appeared, GOD AND BOONE SIGN PERFORMANCE PACT. Next day, HERMAN SLEEPS WITH A TEDDY. Things had gotten crazy. I knew the truth lay somewhere in between. There was no reason to like Herman Boone. He'd taken my job.

BLACK IS BEAUTIFUL

A week later Boone and I met. He introduced himself and I shook his hand. It had a good feel. It was strong and warm. The smile was genuine. The teeth were real. We sat down to talk.

HERE'S THE SCOOP

I knew Boone saw me as a threat. There was no way he couldn't. I'd been picked as "The Guy" and circumstances turned it around. He probably wished I'd quit and taken a job elsewhere. No one likes to be compared with his or her predecessor. I hadn't been in the T.C. Williams job for long but I had a history. Herman Boone was a smart guy. He knew for every Boone lover, there was a Herman hater. Comparisons would be made and issues distorted. He understood he was on a short leash and having Yoast around wouldn't help.

Initially, it was like two bull moose in rutting season. We

were staring each other down before we went on the offensive. The rumor mill never called him a shrinking violet. I'd heard Boone was Delta Force, had hands of stone, and was bad to the bone. I didn't care. I was just a little pissed. I was my own man, I had my own opinions and if he didn't like them, I was ready to rumble.

Now that I've gotten that out of my system, let me be less macho. In my life, for a long time, I've relished the challenge that comes with helping people excel. I've found nothing more rewarding than seeing individuals start low and end high. And that will happen when group enterprise invades the environment. Individual is about you. Leader is about them. If I was leader I also had to be a follower. For years, I preached it and now was the time to live it. So I put my ego in check and opened my arms. Whether I opened my heart was up to him.

At that moment in time the stakes were high. Life and death is serious business. People were being killed in the neighborhood. Our situation was very visible. Race relations aren't a joke. Or football either. Black Coach. White Coach. Will they work together? Can they put their issues aside? Can they set an example for others? To be candid, I'm not sure the school board initially understood the scope and implications of what they had done but I know the community did. It was a pressure cooker. Not only were we charged to win football games but the Hermanator and Honkie were supposed to get along.

The inquisition started gently enough. "So what do you think we need Bill?" I don't think he cared. I say that without malice. Herman Boone was an excellent coach. He'd won the big one. He still had a wife. He knew how to get into the end zone and keep others out. Given his personality he wasn't looking for solutions from me. He had them.

He was thoughtful enough to ask.

There was my opening. My response wouldn't be off the cuff. I had thought about this stuff forever. My mouth was cocked, my lips were greased and the trigger was about to be pulled. It was a long time ago so I can't remember exactly how I unleashed my fury. I do remember it was a monologue.

I wanted him to know that the guy he'd replaced knew as much about coaching as anyone in that room. On many issues my feelings haven't changed. I worshipped integrity at twelve and I worship it today. Experience and age has a way of softening edges but if you really believe in something, it escorts you to the grave. I think my dissertation went something like this—give or take.

I believe that too many coaches or anyone for that matter, involved with the development of people never question what it is that they are charged to do. In the absence of understanding they focus on the superficial. To some, parenting is about food, clothing, and frivolity. To others, coaching involves plays, playmakers and press clippings.

Somewhere, I'd figured out that my job as a coach transcended nothing beyond being the custodian of a person's welfare. Their self-image, happiness, health, prosperity, success, fulfillment and accomplishment were my responsibility. During the time that they were under my supervision if they grew bigger, faster, stronger, and smarter I could take some credit. If the opposite happened, shame on me.

I looked into Herman's face and his expression hadn't changed. I continued.

While I'm pretty sure most people would endorse that statement, talk means nothing. If you, as a coach do not engage in behaviors that turn expectation into reality, you are deficient. If you don't do right by the people you are asking to do right by you, you are a hypocrite.

I was looking for a reaction and there was none. I didn't know why. The words were sliding off my tongue like they had been sprayed with Crisco. When I didn't see crocodile tears erupt from Boone's eyes I started to wonder if he was my kind of guy. I had made a decision to give him my loyalty. Getting my respect would determine whether I remained a Titan or a coach without a team.

It's said wisdom comes with age. Some people get it young and for others it takes a while. In 1971 I guess I wasn't as wise as I thought. Had I been, I would have had a much greater grasp of what the man sitting across from me was thinking.

SOME FACTS

Herman Boone was a black man. He grew up in the south. Only he can fill in the blanks as to what that life entailed. If I were a pie-in-the-sky guy I might suggest that life was B-E-A-U-T-I-F-U-L. If I were Pollyanna I would tell you Boone could swim, run, and jump wherever he pleased. He ate three meals a day and took vitamin supplements. I would suggest opportunity existed everywhere. I would tell you all men and women are created equal and Herman had an equal chance to succeed.

If I told you that I would be dumb and if you believed it you might be dumber. The smarter side of my brain knows it wasn't like that. Books are filled with a history of facts. In Herman Boone's world, you could get hung for saying hello.

At that time I had knowledge about racism, fear, and distrust. I understood how quickly a perception could be created. But I didn't employ it and knowledge without application is like practicing for a game that will never be played. Experience is a wonderful teacher but only if you use the lessons learned.

I don't know why I wasn't teleported back to that cotton field where fifty-eight eyes watched my every move. Two of those eyes could have been Boone's. Bad times have a way of making you suspicious. No wonder he wasn't listening to what I had to say. He was trying to figure out who I was, what I was, and what I might do to him.

I didn't help the situation. In the cotton field I grabbed the dipper and took a sip. But at that moment I was into me. As a result my gums were flapping and all Herman could see was another white guy telling him what to do.

In retrospect I'm surprised he took it as well as he did. Herman asked a lot questions and I responded. When I finished I felt exhausted and energized. I had gotten out those things that were important. If there was a question in Herman's mind about what I believed in, then he couldn't be the guy that taught Einstein how to formulate.

I looked at Boone. There wasn't much of a change but there was enough. I knew that every journey started with a step and I had taken my first with him. His response. "Let's get to work."

A week later the practice season began. The Titans arrived in force. When your high school is as large as a country it takes a day to count. There were big Titans, small Titans, tall Titans, and off-the-wall Titans. The largest guy on the field was in a dress. Another wore bedroom slippers.

The temperature was 98 degrees. For an Alabama cotton picker it was just right. I was up on the field with the assistant coaches. We were getting things organized. It was easy to see who came from where. The GW players were pretty much black and the Hammond players looked like marshmallows. At that point they hadn't become "The Titans." They were just a bunch of young men with attitude problems. They had been exposed to the same rumor mill as everyone else. As a result, the white guys didn't like the black guys and the black guys didn't like the white guys. Herman had not yet arrived. When he finally showed up, I was happy with my decision to stay with him. He was an equal opportunity coach. Boone didn't like anybody.

He had a new whistle and sparkling shoes. Beautiful cap. His shorts were starched and his frown was too. He appeared to be a nine feet tall but if you cut the afro that had grown wild on his head, Boone was around six feet. He wasn't a dominant physical force but what he lacked in size he made up for in personality. When Herman was Hermanizing he got your attention.

I've been asked to describe Boone. My response— prickly pear with a turbo charger on his lips. That was okay.

If you could navigate the thorns to get to the meat, it was pretty sweet.

I suspect he was born with a high-octane personality and circumstances elevated it. Boone had clawed his way to the top by being tough and there aren't many people who discard what got them to the party. I had no problem with that.

I even thought maybe I could learn something from Herman. I knew I'd have to ignore the delivery and pay attention to the content. I figured I could put my stuff with his stuff and create a little synergy.

On the first day of practice there was so much organizing going on I wasn't paying any attention to Herman. I had my own problems. But on the second day, I heard Boone on his bullhorn trying to get a player's attention. The *Guinness Book of World Records* should have been there. I'd never heard anything like it. In one sentence Herman Boone put fifty-three words together and fifty-two of them were profane. The reaction was astonishing. In three seconds, the player that had been muddling around fell into ranks and stood at attention. I was impressed. I was amazed.

That night I went home and tried to adopt Boone's technique. There was no question I was an amateur. I couldn't remember ever having used a swear word. I'm sure I did but the memory was lost. I stood in front of the mirror and took a deep breath. My face contorted. I clenched my fist and raised it in the air. My foot twitched. I was ready and I would start with the lord's name in vain. Timing had to be perfect. It was all in the technique.

I had butterflies in my stomach. Here we go. My arm

crashed down as the words erupted from my mouth. "Gosh darn it," I screamed. I decided to try the F-word. "Fiddle-sticks," broke the silence. Maybe the S-word would get me going. "Shucks," I yelled. "Son of a beeswax. Dadnabbit, go to heck."

Yeah, Herman and I had differences and some of them would remain.

As time went on I had a feeling that the team was getting better even though the atmosphere was getting worse. There were lots of reasons and one was that Herman was a hard man to be around. He was an in your face rock-'em sock-'em coach and no different in personality than Vince Lombardi, Bill Parcels, or Bull Halsey—three leaders among many that got results and never won a personality contest. I didn't hold that against him. A few assistant coaches did. Some quit and the ones that remained had an attitude that you could cut with a knife. In search of answers Herman identified me as the problem. He knew many of the coaches had worked for me and he figured I had poisoned them against him. He reported me to the athletic director and assistant superintendent.

I don't know exactly what he said but they called me in to explain what was going on. I was hot. I was insulted at the suggestion that I would conspire against him. I told them if I had a problem with Herman I would address it with him. They suggested I should. I did and behind many closed doors Herman and I talked it out. We came to the conclusion that our coaching styles were different. I explained I was more like Tom Landry. Herman responded that having an emotional telephone pole for an assistant would be okay. It wasn't his way but he was willing to accept it. I asked him who he thought his style mirrored. He gave it some thought. I think he said, "I'm a cross between Martin Luther King and Godzilla." The smile I expected to see never came. This journey was going to be interesting. What we both knew was that we wanted the Titans to win and that was reason enough to change.

He compromised. I compromised. Things got better. The Titans got better but there were still real issues. Racism and hatred don't disappear with a touchdown pass. At that point, the team was not a team. It was collection of talented cliques. Not surprising, each had its own color. Herman coached the offense and I coached the defense. Gerry Bertier was my anchor and also the captain of the team. I was always looking for Bertier to provide some leadership. Unfortunately, his dominant presence and porcupine disposition did not make others want to cuddle.

One day it seemed that every player was going after every other player. The whistle would blow indicating that the action should stop and guys were still blocking, tackling, and throwing elbows. Two players had taken it to a higher level. Surprising in that they were on the same side. Both played defense. When practice ended I called Gerry Bertier and Julius Campbell over and marched them into the bleachers. I exploded with a tirade that would have made Boone proud. I told them I thought they both might be racists. I then added that I couldn't do anything about how they felt but I could do something about how they acted and if they didn't cut out the BS something was going to happen. A few days later it did.

Hatred is ubiquitous and it's not about hugs and kisses. Three troublemakers decided they could build a reputation by taking Bertier out. One afternoon as Gerry crossed the school parking lot he was jumped. I'm not sure what they were thinking but they greatly underestimated their prey. Within moments Bertier had pounded them into submission. As he was wiping their jive off his knuckles, Julius Campbell stumbled upon the scene. Julius knew the guys were bad dudes. He was impressed. He might not like Bertier but he had to respect his punching power.

The next day Julius arrived at practice and announced he had a story to tell. The team assembled around him. This story was about Superman. As he said the word, he pointed to Bertier. At least fifty-eight eyes turned in Bertier's direction.

One act by one man had changed a perception. He might not be black but he was okay. The team had found its leader and he was no rhinestone cowboy. The logic followed. With Superman at the helm, the Titans had a future.

They were right. We went undefeated and won the state championship. We not only took home the trophy, we dominated virtually every team we played. Seven of the ten regular season games were shutouts. Our competition averaged 113 yards per game during the season.

The Titans averaged 319. We scored 266 points to our competitor's 31. In the playoffs we scored 91 points to the competition's 14. Our excellence was underscored in the

State Championship game against Andrew Lewis High School. They didn't score and their offense was held to minus five yards.

Were the Titans superhuman kids? Far from it. If you took a look at the rosters you would see that we were smaller than many of the teams we played. There is nothing novel in a smaller team dominating a bigger team. We did it in Virginia but I can tell you, it happens everywhere.

It was a dream season. The Titans had come a long way. We set a goal and achieved it. I decided it was time to move on. For me it didn't matter that I wasn't moving up. I'd never had much of an ego. Great expectations were for Pip. When you start life in a cotton field you don't look beyond getting promoted to the watermelon patch.

Even though I was coaching at T. C. Williams I was still teaching at Hammond. They had a J.V. team and that was fine. I knew the players and they were great. If I could help them achieve something that would be enough. I've always believed the earlier you impact a kid the more you can do for them. I think the guys who coach Pop Warner understand the concept. I left.

I don't know how Herman Boone took my resignation. On the one hand I'm sure he was disappointed to lose an effective coach, on the other, he recognized we were very different people. Our philosophy and style of coaching were often at odds. In the course of getting through the season there were numerous times when conflict came to Titanville. I'm an easy-going guy and I've always believed that it helps if you ride a horse in the direction it's going. Herman was going his way and I decided to go mine.

I took my program home. Glenn Furman made a decision to go with me. We had been together for years and fit like a banana and peel. The venue would be smaller but that didn't matter. The kids would be the same. Our personalities were a compliment. In some ways Glenn was my alter ego. I was quiet and he was loud. I was methodical and Furman was impulsive. I was a lava lamp and Glenn was Quasar. Between the two of us we covered the spectrum. I provided the ambiance and Furman lit the fire. I guess it worked. Over the next few years, coaching everything, our program went 64-1. We had a thirty-eight game winning streak.

One day I was told Hammond would shrink again. Football would be replaced by hopscotch. The next day my phone rang. I picked it up. It was Boone. He was mellow. I figured he'd popped a Prozac. An invitation was extended. If you're a coach you need a team. I said yes and so did Glenn. We became Titans once more. The year was 1974. In 1980 I left to assist a friend in getting a program started. It worked.

Two years later Herman retired. Two years after that Glenn Furman was given the Titan head coach job. He'd earned it. He called and asked if I would help. He knew the answer. A role reversal was taking a place and what a compliment. There is no greater satisfaction than knowing that someone you mentored is now better than you. When they want you to be a part of their future it punctuates the point that he or she valued what you gave them.

Glenn Furman inherited a losing program. He turned it around in one year. Over the next ten seasons the "Furman Assault Force" went 96-21-2 and won eight district titles, four regional titles and two state championships. In 1984 they were 14-0 and were ranked third in the nation by *USA Today*. They were also picked as the Metropolitan Team of the Decade. In 1985 they were the state runner-up. In 1987 they produced another 14-0 season and were ranked 7th in the nation. Furman was selected as the Washington Metropolitan Coach of the Year three times. He was a Virginia coach of the year and voted into the Fairfax County Football Coaches Hall of Fame.

At the end, I watched with great pride. Three decades earlier I had taken a brash twenty-year-old biology teacher with a big heart, loud mouth, and marginal judgment and gave him a chance. Thirty years later Glenn Furman had become a star.

NO MAGIC

There is a saying, "know thyself." When you know yourself you can be yourself. When you don't know who you are you might try to be someone else. In the coaching business and life it never works. I didn't always know who I was. I didn't know being myself was important. Early on in my coaching career I wanted to be like Lombardi. I wanted to be rough and tough. I wanted to intimidate. Then I read an article about a well-known coach. In this exposé, he was described as "punishing, intimidating, and explosive." You had to feel sympathy for the players. His dictatorial style got results but at what expense? Did he win because of what he did or in spite of it? I knew the answer. I also understood the association between how you are treated and what you become.

It's incredible in this era of enlightenment how many people haven't gotten the word. There are those that still believe a bullying style of leading is conducive to producing results. The failure of countless teams where a despot called the plays would indicate otherwise.

After that article I recognized I could never be that kind of coach and it didn't matter because results could be achieved other ways. Sure Lombardi was great but so was Susan Jones and she was quiet and soft spoken. When Susan was around you might not notice. There was no huffing and puffing, no threats and no fists in the face. She didn't wear jackboots and a spiked helmet. But that didn't mean her plan wasn't solid. She just found a different way to implement it. I suspect if Vince attempted to ride his personality horse in the opposite direction I wouldn't be mentioning him now.

I might as well stop here and tell you I am a student of history. I read a great deal and pay attention to what others have done in getting followers to higher levels of accomplishment. There is nothing cryptic in a leader-follower relationship. The things that motivated players a thousand years ago are appropriate today. Have you ever read the techniques that got Solomon through a tough day? They weren't much different than what Knute Rockne used to bring it home for the Gipper. Because coaching and leading have so many parallels, when I refer to a coach I could just as easily say leader.

There are those that have complicated the process of coaching. I've been to the clinics. I've heard the speeches. I've invested in the literature. Some of it has been excellent and much of it hasn't. Whenever I find myself disagreeing with the input, I recognize it is because the expert has elevated form over substance.

They seem to discount the part emotion plays in winning and losing. They've captured the science of getting a strategy down but have left out the art of getting a player up.

Formulas don't win games but minds do. Coaches that lose have players that say, "I can't" and those that win have players that say, "I must."

This doesn't happen by accident and it may take a few years of fits and starts to get the recipe right. I believe there are countless things that get a team into the victory circle and the vast majority of them having nothing to do with you.

There was a time when I was a "hands on" guy. If things were going to happen I would have to be involved. The responsibility for the team was mine so it didn't seem unreasonable to hold the bridle tight. I don't remember if it was by accident or design but at some point when I loosened up, things improved. A light ignited.

I figured out my job, as the leader, was not to dominate the situation, but rather facilitate the process. In coaching, just as in the universe, there is a natural order of things. Much about coaching is letting the process evolve on its own. Too many cooks spoil the soup and too much instruction can ruin a kid. I once drew a parallel between coaching and surveying. My job was to establish the operational boundaries. As a player you had leeway as long as you met my performance criteria:

- ◆ You will show up on time.
- ◆ You will work hard.
- ◆ You will pay attention.
- ◆ You will be a team player.

I believe in quid pro quo so that meant there were criteria for me:

- I would show up on time.
- I would work hard.
- I would pay attention.
- I would be a team player.

That's right. I was part of the team. I was not above the team. Doing what I expected from others just seemed right. The perception your players have of you is critical to the coach-player relationship and if they think you don't live your sermon they will not only question who you are but everything you tell them.

For me, the team represented all those elements that had an impact on success: coaches, faculty, trainers, cheerleaders, and fans. There was the team that played, there was the team that instructed and there was the team that supported.

As a coach, you have a large constituency and it is your responsibility to create harmony among the different elements. One detractor can ruin your day. I'm sure that's why a number of coaches have described their job as akin to a conductor. They don't want to play the trombone; they just want to hear some perfect notes. One of the greatest coaches of all-time, John Wooden, understood the concept. So does Bill Billichek. If you're wondering how Southwest Airlines became the king of the skies you should see how Herb Kelleher works his baton.

And then there was Bob Atkins. What a coach! He saw his job as that of a servant. Why not? He was asking his athletes to perform on his behalf. He was demanding hard work, sacrifice, and abstinence. He wanted much from the girls he guided. For him it seemed reasonable that he should give something back. He'd be happy to run an errand, carry your shoes, or get you some water. If you fell, Bob was the first one there with a Band-Aid. I never saw a request go unfulfilled. We coached together, roomed together, and shared a friendship. He was black and I was white. We both were colorblind. Bob is gone but the memories are fresh. In the years that he and I worked together, I got to witness how a great man could be humble and in his humility he inspired everyone he touched.

Facilitating the process involves embracing the attitude that you are only half as smart as you think.

If you believe you don't have all the answers, you'll go looking for them and they will show up in the most unusual places. Coaches who facilitate the process see everyone as a resource and every situation as an opportunity to learn.

GO WEST!

Lewis and Clark understood the concept. In the annals of American history there may be no better example of leadership or the display of leadership principles than what is chronicled in their expedition log.

At the request of Thomas Jefferson, Meriwether Lewis and William Clark were to take a group of intrepid explorers and document everything they encountered in their journey from St. Louis to parts unknown. In the course of their travels they would encounter innumerable obstacles that would challenge the essence of their ability. Incredibly, they overcame every adversity. A year and a half after leaving St. Louis, they found themselves on the northwest Pacific coast, with winter approaching. Short on provisions and eager to report back to Jefferson they contemplated what to do—return to St. Louis or stay put until spring. The decision had life-threatening consequences. Assembled by a roaring fire, the matter was opened for discussion. Every possibility was reviewed and yet Lewis and Clark could not make a decision. They decided to take a vote. Majority ruled. Everyone would participate. Everyone! Even Sacagawea, the Shoshone Indian they had retained as an interpreter.

I suspect a couple of lesser leaders would have disenfranchised her. She didn't have the look. Talked with an accent. Lacked credentials. Wore a deerskin dress.

Lewis and Clark thought otherwise. They understood when venturing into unknown territory every resource is important. And as a result, their expedition is now ranked as one of the greatest accomplishments in American history.

When you retire the "know it all" attitude, you open up a world of possibilities. There is nothing wrong with questioning what you are doing. If it's right you'll validate it and if it's wrong you'll discover the error in your thinking. When you seek input and criticism you have changed nothing. You will become aware of what already exists.

One of the great leaders in American industry in the twentieth century was the CEO of Intel, Andy Grove. He wrote a terrific book about his company thriving because of paranoia.

I was going through an airport one day and it caught my eye. I owned some Intel stock and couldn't believe my CEO was paranoid. Sybil was paranoid. Rasputin was paranoid. Richard Nixon was paranoid. But Andy Grove? I had to buy it to see if I should dump the stock.

The concept behind his dissertation was if you aren't paranoid you are never examining what you're doing. You are never looking over your shoulder. One day you awaken and the "boogieman" has taken you down. Paranoia forces you to constantly evaluate where you are. And it is that assessment that ultimately makes you better.

I guess I've always been a little paranoid. Maybe insecure is a better word. The formative years had an impact and mine were anything but ego building. I have regrets but then I can also see the upside. When I knew I didn't have the answer I turned to others for help.

Early on, I thought I could identify who was an asset. I figured I could spot the talent. What I've learned over the years is that I've seldom been able to determine who can get the job done until I've given them an opportunity to perform. Facilitating the process means everyone gets a chance because it is opportunity that is the catalyst for performance. People who have never been given an opportunity are thirsty for a chance. When it comes, they have been known to seize the moment and perform at astonishing levels. Juvenile delinquents have become Medal of Honor winners. The down and out have risen to greatness.

I'LL TAKE THEM ALL

Building a team involves capturing the collective talent of a group: big ones, small ones, dark ones, tall ones. Throw in some thick heads and smarts guys as well. Diversity means you will employ a cross section of talent.

My daughter Angela moved to California. She fell in love with an oil field worker. They moved back to Virginia and because there was no black gold, he found himself unemployed. Rick Garrison had initiative so he went to plumbing school. Whenever they came over he talked about plumbing and pipes. I yawned. I wanted to discuss FOOT-BALL! I was about ready to ask Angela to trade him in when a major winter storm hit the area. My pipes froze and burst. The Virginia Plumbers Association estimated a week. Five minutes later the most beautiful guy on earth showed up and fixed the problem.

I still fall prey to stereotypes. I forget that a lot of people are acting. I still believe I can spot the winner. And then when I least expect it, I'm surprised again. I was on a speaking tour when I stumbled into a restaurant. I had few hours to kill and thought I might do a little sight seeing. I didn't know much about the area so I figured I'd get some input from a local expert. There he stood next to the cash register: Physically fit, clean-cut, expensive shoes, beautiful tie, and Armani suit. He was obviously an intelligent businessman. I approached and asked if he could give me some information. A frown appeared, a vacant sign showed up in his eyes. He confessed he knew nothing. He was innocent. He pleaded for me to retract my question. His mother told him not to talk to strangers. He asked if he could be excused.

I granted the request.

A teenager sitting in a booth nearby heard my question. In an instant she was in my face—purple hair, no suit, sandals, beads, a spike through her nose and tattoo on her cheek. "What do you need to know?" she asked. I was a little intimidated. I was innocent. Thank God my mom had told me to talk to strangers. I gave her my request and she gave me back an encyclopedia worth of information. Once again I'd been fooled.

I've been fooled so many times I now have an operational directive.

Ignore First Impressions!

They're seldom accurate and always incomplete. When I joined the Air Commandos I remember standing in formation. I looked to the left. I thought it was a casting call for *Beach Blanket Bingo*. Beautiful dudes and muscles too. I gazed to the right. How'd they get in? I wondered. I knew who would make the cut. I was wrong. On graduation day everyone wanted the commandos to fight but no one wanted a picture. Experience has taught me more often than not that people are the inverse of their facade. So now I'm a "show me" kind of guy. If you're acting, I'll find out.

When you facilitate the process you open up communication.

As a coach you will always be venturing into unfamiliar territory. The good news is what is unknown to you, is known to someone else. One brain is good. Many brains are better. Listen up. Pay attention. Don't take offense that someone is trying to help. Their motive may be noble. Their input may be accurate. Accept it, digest it, let it ferment, and then put it under a microscope. If you find it's healthy, employ it and if not, put it in your cerebral storage shed for another time. On occasion you may want to flush it away.

When you assume a leadership position you can't help but have biases. It's part of being human. Just keep those biases in check. Adopt an attitude that everything is fair game. Encourage access. Solicit feedback. When you do, everyone will know that you view them as an asset and they will become one.

One of our toughest competitors over the years was Washington and Lee High School The school drew from a large area and as a result they always had talent and size. They also played a wide six defense. In that formation, the defensive tackle lined up against the offensive guard. In Jimmy Locher's case it meant he was trying to block a 250 pound behemoth. For all his desire, it wasn't working. He suggested we flip the guard and tackle. That way our big tackle would block their big tackle. In a wide six there was no one on the tackle so he would be free to block a linebacker. I had trouble making the adjustment because my mind was in a rut. I was handcuffed to the past. Thank goodness he was a salesman and convinced me to try it. I did and it worked beautifully. We won the game and from then on, every time I encountered a wide six I employed the "Locher Plan."

Was Jimmy Locher responsible for us winning the Regional Championship? What do you think?

I learned from that experience and employed the knowledge a few years later. It was the beginning of the Titan season and there were a number of reasons why I wasn't the most popular coach around. One of them had to do with color. A number of our Titans hung with the Black Panthers and had adopted an attitude that white wasn't even good on milk. I was the defensive coach and having one of my stars, Julius Campbell, think I was the devil was no way to bond.

Julius was a terrific player but had an attitude that stunk. One day watching game films I asked Julius what he thought. He turned to me and grumbled something about why would I care what he thought. I told him he was a smart guy and I needed his help.

A few days later on the practice field he came up and asked if I was serious about wanting his input. I responded that I did. He gave me a mouthful. I employed some of it and it worked. I got results and turned my naysayer into an advocate.

One year I had a running back that I thought was terrific. Statistics proved differently. At the end of the season I sat down with him and we tried to figure out what was wrong. We determined my play calling did not suit his running style. It was too specific. He was a dutiful follower. When the play called for him to hit the hole, he did. Just as instructed. If the hole was filled he went nowhere. When the season was over he finally spoke up. There must have been something in my coaching style that inhibited his input earlier on. He asked me if I would just let him go where he saw daylight. I thought that was a good idea. The next season I told him he was free to go wherever he wanted. It was in his hands. That season ended and he had become one of the top rushers in the state.

I facilitated the process by doing nothing more than letting him do what he knew best. I've been punished when I denied people freedom and I've been rewarded when I took the bridle off.

Lots of kids get in trouble as they enter their teens. All their lives their parents were in charge. They were told what to do and how to do it and for good reason. You don't learn in a vacuum. But at some point after those lessons have been learned and knowledge gained, a child wants to experiment. They are ready to make their own decisions. If you don't let them, at best you inhibit growth but even worse, you set the stage for rebellion.

Patrick Henry understood the importance of freedom. If he couldn't have it he'd rather be dead.

In coaching, you teach your athletes what to do but at some point they have to do it on their own. They have to make decisions. When you interject yourself into every scenario you take away their ability to think and I've never seen a thoughtless athlete take home the gold.

Facilitating the process means influencing the proper perceptions.

Perception is everything. In the relationship-building business, perception governs conduct. Who you are is one thing. What people think you are is more important. People respond to what they see. Perception is the driving force behind behavior. Recognize that you may know who you are but others don't. Most people carry a basket of suspicions. For good reasons. Their life before you was not a walk on the yellow brick road. Anyone who has been mistreated, betrayed, or let down remembers it.

In leading a team, when you exhibit the same behaviors you seek in others you'll create an impression you're okay. If you want discipline, courage, honesty, teamwork, dedication, and loyalty, you should display discipline, courage, honesty, teamwork, dedication, and loyalty.

I'm not sure why so many leaders struggle with the concept. For me, doing what I wanted done always made sense. It's tough getting to any championship. The pain, the suffering, the hardship are an ever-present reality. Frequently your players will question the essence of the person who introduced the misery. If you have influenced the proper perceptions they will come to the conclusion that you ask no more of them than you demand of yourself.

Facilitating the process means building confidence.

When I first started coaching I didn't understand the power of confidence. I wanted to make my players stronger, faster, and smarter. As an empirical guy I liked the fact that those attributes could be measured. Confidence was intangible. I knew it was important but wasn't sure why. I never would have guessed that a principle component of my coaching philosophy would come as the result of lemonade.

I'm sure you've noticed every summer the entrepreneurial spirit is born. Across America a million kids convince mom to help them earn gum money. On the surface, there doesn't appear to be all that much to it. Some may think that but others have a different understanding. A friend told me a story.

The first time his kids went out to sell lemonade he realized there were issues at play that transcended making a buck. In reality, selling lemonade is a very big deal. It's about quality, salesmanship, delivery, distribution, and pricing. Selling lemonade is about success and failure. The last thing he wanted his kids to experience was the rejection that was felt when you complete a three-hour tour of duty and your pitcher is full. He decided to eliminate the possibility of that happening. It was pretty easy. His kids sat on the sidewalk and he positioned himself around the corner five blocks away. Every potential customer that was moving in their direction was stopped and given a quarter to buy a cup. Everyone was excited to participate. Who wouldn't want to get free lemonade and help a kid too? They understood who was going to pay their Social Security. An hour went by and he decided to see what his kids were doing. As he walked up he could see the enthusiasm on their faces. They were excited. They were yelling. They were jumping. They were winning. He attributes that the confidence they gained on that day helped set a foundation to a lifetime of success. It cost him $7.25 and it was the best investment he ever made.

I know that there are people who might hear that story and question the merit of the father's actions. They might say if there was no failure, that's not the real world. Some might suggest if the kids found out that their dad had a hand in their success, they would believe their success was a sham.

I guess there are lots of ways to look at anything. There was a time I overplayed the "what if" game—upside, downside, inside, outside. And when I did I could always find a reason for doing nothing. I no longer do. I now use one criterion. I ask myself whether my action will make someone better. If the answer is yes, I do it. If I erred in my assessment I correct the situation and move on.

As a coach, my responsibility is to help people improve. The process is linear. Winning starts with preparation: physical, mental, and emotional. It's followed with application. People who are prepared want to apply their new ability. Let them. Help them.

Now here is where you earn your pay. You decide where and when that application takes place. The object is to generate success because success builds confidence and confidence is the accelerant. Confidence is the flash point for momentum. Momentum is a precursor for victory.

Once the victory is achieved, the third step kicks in: recognition. You applaud the achievement. You highlight the effort. You praise the dedication. You run it up the flagpole. You hand out a medal. Buy a plaque. Put a star on a helmet. What's important is that you acknowledge the achievement because people respond to praise. Praise builds confidence. More praise more confidence. More confidence more success. More success more confidence. Linear becomes circular. Get the process started and it feeds on itself.

If you don't remember the statistic in the 1971 State Championship game here it is again. The second best team in the state of Virginia had minus five yards against the Titans. Confidence dominated the day. Building confidence has always been at the core of my coaching philosophy. It's so fundamental to winning that I've never understood why anyone would attempt to diminish a player. I know it can happen by accident.

As a coach you have a bag of psychological tools at your disposal. If you're any good, you use the right tool at the appropriate time. It's not an exact science but with practice and experience you'll hit the mark more often than not. I've tried to make players feel proud, I've attempted to generate a feeling of guilt, I've made them question their dedication and inspect their loyalty. But the one thing I won't do is tear someone down. Nobody excels when feeling low. When you destroy confidence you contaminate the fuel that ignites the spirit. You remove the catalyst for self-esteem. You handcuff the governor of excellence. After years of fits and starts it finally came to me. Confidence is a critical performance driver and it will make the difference between winning a championship or watching one.

There are a few things you need to know about confidence:

♦ Confidence Is Combustible

It was one of the most arduous mountain climbing legs in the Tour de France. Lance Armstrong had been struggling getting up the mountain. As the camera panned to his face you could see the agony that reflected the fire in his legs. The camera showcased his number one competitor who looked a third as tired and twice as strong. At this point in the tour many of the newscasters believed Lance's days in the sun were over. As he moved up the mountain, his bike came precariously close to a fan standing on the side of the road. Something caught Armstrong's handlebars and he and his bike were wrenched to the ground. Everyone watching was in shock. Because the Tour de France is won by seconds, a newscaster proclaimed that the end of Armstrong had come. Lance didn't become Lance by accident. He had a reservoir of courage that was bottomless. Somehow, within seconds, bruised and bleeding he was on the go. As he began to pass his competitors something marvelous happened. His confidence was ignited. The pain vanished from his face as the energy erupted in his body. He blew by riders as if they were standing still. Some believe it was the greatest comeback in cycling history. Armstrong went on to win his fifth Tour de France. Confidence was the generator that shot him up the mountain.

What happened with Lance is not unique. Since the beginning confidence has played a role in victory. For as long as people have attempted to excel, confidence has been at the core. History records incredible feats. Confidence was that inner voice that whispered to "get in the ring" and then commanded to "stay there." Because of confidence less became more and wannabe's became winners. When confidence is present anything is possible.

♦ Confidence Is Infectious

Because confidence is a state of mind when it erupts it travels at the speed of thought.

Remember the 1993 Super Bowl? Both teams got there by winning. Both teams were confident. The Buffalo Bills had made it four times. Rightly so, they were being called one of the greatest teams in NFL history. Their talent was immense and their egos huge. In a pre-game interview standing next to the announcer they looked awesome.

After the game only one was a winner. The Bills were called "losers." They weren't losers; they just hadn't won. Not surprisingly, after being chastised for their loss, they started to show the psychological effects. In four quarters they had morphed from athletic giants into a dispirited dwarfs. They seemed small and insignificant. They were apologetic. They were sad. I felt pity. The next season they were not themselves. As matter of fact, they haven't been themselves since 1993.

For a long time I've known that confidence turns meek into mighty. On that day, I learned that confidence was a double-edged sword. I've seen similar situations. What I continue to marvel at is the speed at which it happens. I've come to the conclusion:

♦ Confidence Is Fragile

Guard it, protect it, shelter it, and defend it. Confidence is breakable and when it has been broken the mighty become the meek.

Facilitating the process involves developing your players.

Most people have a self-centered interpretation of reality. As a result, they have imposed an artificial ceiling on their ability. They can't help it. It comes from going through life in their skin. Your job is to introduce them to a new reality. It took me a long time to figure that out. My only excuse is that I wasn't developed. Learning is an evolutionary thing and comes from experience. The more you get, the better you are.

It doesn't matter who they are. If you want to take them to a higher level of performance they need to be developed. I've never met a leader that wouldn't say making their team better was a priority. Even the most unenlightened would agree that when people have more skill and capability they can perform better. Unfortunately, what many profess as their philosophy does not show up on the videotape. They believe that development is crucial and yet their actions run counter to their attitude.

I recently heard a coach proclaim that, "He was hired to win football games. He was not a baby sitter. Behavior off the field was an individual's responsibility." He walked his talk and as a result, his team imploded. Had he introduced a program that highlighted civic responsibility, there would have been no victims, a few lives would have been salvaged, and he would still have his job.

Over the years I've seen an abundance of kids that needed help. It should have been given long before they got to me. I remember one parent who had no money for a tutor but was always flush when someone shouted "beer."

What should be understood is that there are consequences when someone is not properly developed. That parent may be giving milk money to a fifty year old. The concept is so fundamental why wouldn't anyone develop the talent they had? I've come to the conclusion that there are a few reasons:

- It takes time to develop people.
- There is an expense in developing people.
- There is ignorance as to who needs to be developed and what needs to be done.

In every environment there are people who are not prepared to do their best. Did you know that they know it? They would like to fix it. I believe development is an inalienable right. As a coach I am asking for my players help. Quid pro quo demands if I ask for it, I should be willing to give it. And the sooner I do, the quicker the individual will improve.

Whenever I've taken on a leadership responsibility I don't tiptoe into the environment. I hold a huddle. I ask some questions. I make some claims. The first thing I do is build expectation. I want everyone to know they will get better. I found that expectation creates optimism. When people believe they are going to improve they get excited. Excitement is a catalyst for effort and it is effort that makes the difference.

Some people don't get it. Not the fact that there are weak links. Everyone understands that. Anyone who has ever lead a team acknowledges the weakness exists. Knowing it is one thing, accepting it is something else. No leader of any consequence has ever blessed having marginal guys in the middle. The difference between a leader and someone that should take up following lies not in the identification of the deficiency but rather the speed at which you do something about it.

He was the commanding officer of the 82nd Airborne Division and some said as fine a leader as America ever produced. In 1989 he went to war and never left. Name the conflict and Swannack was there. When trouble ignited Chuck Swannack was called on to extinguish the flames. Airborne, Ranger, Jungle Expert. His chest was filled with medals. Everyone who had ever met General Swannack knew he was as hard as a woodpecker's lips.

But it wasn't his toughness that made his leadership extraordinary. It was his uncompromising commitment to the welfare of others. His mission had always centered around making his soldiers the best that they could be. The amazing thing was that Chuck Swannack applied that same attitude to people he didn't know. A request was made. The timing was bad. General Swannack had his hands full dodging bullets and facing the challenges that come with great responsibility. It didn't matter. A little boy needed help and he felt obliged to give it. The letter read:

Joe,
I received your email address yesterday but I was a bit busy closing out a battle here in Iraq. I was told you asked about the war and what keeps soldiers together. Every week I speak to all the newly assigned troopers in the 82nd Airborne Division, and the points I always discuss are DSWAT . . . Discipline, Skill, Will and Teamwork! It is the philosophy by which I command soldiers.

Discipline is "always doing what is right" in the absence of orders or someone telling you what to do.

Skill is physical as well as technical—physical fitness, ability to use your weapon, airborne proficiency, buddy first aid, and small unit tactical drills.

Will is a positive attitude to accomplish the task at hand even when confronted with problems or adversity.

Teamwork is to always be a contributing member to whatever team you are assigned.

I tell all the troopers that we follow the Golden Rule and treat each other with dignity and respect. Additionally, we all have an airborne buddy to take care of and keep safe. Over here, I challenge every trooper to bring their buddy home alive.

I close by telling the troopers why I demand DSWAT from every member of the 82nd Airborne Division. It is because lives depend daily on the discipline, skill, will and teamwork of others. This philosophy proves true every day here in combat and every day back at Ft Bragg, too.

Apply DSWAT to your life Joe and I think you will find it will make a difference.

All the Way . . . Airborne!
MG Chuck Swannack

I was honored to have been shown that letter. I know why General Swannack wrote it. People don't get better by accident.

Facilitating the process means being fair.

When I first started coaching I viewed all my players the same. I was a fan of Jefferson and he had said people were created equal. It makes for a hot headline. In reality it's off the mark. Genetics makes everyone unequal. Parenting, environment, and experience widens the gap. Throw in some mistrust, apprehension, and a wiggle in your walk and the group that shows up on the first day of practice is inherently unequal.

There are players that are rough and tough and others whose knees are knocking. There are those that are sharp as razors and some as dull as mud. The emotional make-up of your team will run the gamut from titanium to egg shells. And this is why they call you coach. It is your responsibility to evaluate the potential of each individual and then help him or her realize it.

There was a time I tried to treat everyone equally. I raised the performance bar and told people to get over it. For some it was too low and for others it was too high. The high potential athlete felt underchallenged and the low potential player felt diminished when the bar cracked him in the nose. In both cases I lost.

It was the 1968 season and I was feeling pretty good about myself. During the summer practice sessions I rode my guys hard. One young man, Jack Coogan, didn't care for it. At 325 pounds he was the biggest guy on the field. After a series of forty-yard sprints Jack asked if he could be excused to go to the bathroom. He never returned.

The next season Jack came out again. Same drill. Summer workouts were meant for suffering. Everyone would run and everyone would feel the pain. Jack had gotten a year older and a bit more confident. He decided to speak up. He asked if he could show me something. I said okay. He dropped his pants and pointed to his inner thighs. They were blistered, blood red, and oozed pain. He had rubbed them raw. "I can't do the sprints coach." My first reaction was to tell Jack to suck it up but then I realized he might want to take another visit to the bathroom.

I stood there and surveyed the wounds. Anybody who could have lasted as long as he did wasn't a wimp. Jack might have been as tough a player as we had but he was operating under different circumstances.

On that day enlightenment penetrated my thick skull. People were not equal. Everyone had their strengths and their weaknesses. There were differences. To treat everyone the same was profoundly stupid and blatantly unfair. We had a number of heavy players that fell into the Coogan category. I adjusted. I made wind sprints optional. I came up with a few other drills that got the desired results. The problem went away and Jack Coogan became a dominant player and an All-Metro selection. In retrospect, I wonder why it took me so long to figure that out.

The epiphany arrived and I changed. When I did, I transformed a dropout into a star. The lesson was learned. My success would hinge on my ability to elevate the performance bar to the right level. Placement was the key. I've learned that there is nothing wrong with asking a player what they thought. Their input plus my capability analysis determined how high we would go. When I allowed my player to be part of the process, every challenge was met with success and every success became an energizing force.

I'm not the first person that has figured this out. Any coach of consequence understands the deal. That's why bad teams have been fixed overnight and great teams have been destroyed in the same amount of time. Fletcher Christian was a terrific team player and then one day he said, "I quit."

When he did, half a team went with him. Bligh was never the same.

To make sure I treated people fairly, I began to break my players down into three categories.

The Blue Chipper. This is the player that has it all. He or she is not hard to spot. They are key to championships. Keep raising the bar until they tell you they have had enough. Take a break and then raise it again. No matter what you demand of a Blue Chipper, he or she will attempt to get it done.

My assistant coach, Glenn Furman understood the concept. We were in the playoffs and had our hands full with a very tough team. Our star defensive end got injured and came to the sidelines. The next down was critical. Furman had the answer. He turned to John O'Connor and told him to go in and play the position. The only problem was this Blue Chipper was our quarterback and had never played a down on defense. He was glad to accommodate his coach. As O'Connor ran onto the field I stood in shock. Our franchise was about to vanish. He rushed the passer, knocked the ball free and recovered the fumble. He turned his jersey around and then took us into the end zone.

The Plugger. This player has not been fully developed but has substantial potential. The Plugger has been underutilized and knows it. The Plugger has been waiting for you to make them better. When your developmental plan takes a Plugger from operating at 40 percent to 65 percent, that gain is significant. Now multiply that number by the number of Plug-

gers on the team and all of a sudden you're in a ticker tape parade.

The Kantby. The Kantby does not possess the skill or capability to do what needs to be done. These are the people that you need to point in a different direction. Life is not fair, but you can be. You can also be sensitive and kind as you explain why the situation may not be right for them. Some of the most productive people on the planet were playing in the wrong arena and when they were encouraged to go somewhere else, they rewrote the record book.

When I began to establish "acceptable" performance points based upon potential, I got better results. When I treated people fairly they not only performed at a higher level but also had a better attitude. When people fail they are disappointed. They search for answers. They scrutinize behavior. They wonder if they were treated right. You'll become the target of their inquisition. Thumbs up or thumbs down. If you have treated people fairly they know it and with that knowledge they will let you play another day.

Facilitating the process means telling it like it is.

Too many people struggle with the concept. I think the foundation for deceit begins in childhood. One day you awaken and begin to question the world around you. You want answers. Why doesn't the fat guy in the red suit use the front door? How can the reindeer get full on two cookies and a stick of celery? Does Santa outsource? The charade continues. The suspicions mount. Why doesn't the tooth

fairy adjust for inflation? Where does the Easter Bunny get the chocolate? Facts are not forthcoming and you remain confused. If you're lucky, some cold-hearted bastard gives it to you straight. "Your mom ate the cookies."

We cannot open the paper, turn on the television, or surf the Internet without being exposed to someone in trouble because of communication or a lack thereof. The "straight scoop" is critical to elevating performance. I've discovered candor is productive. I've learned that people want the truth. Sooner is better. Prolonging the inevitable wastes time and squanders resources. Both are hard to come by. Hiding the facts has never served anyone well—at least not in the long term. Make the assessment, deliver the goods and then get on with what has to be done.

Facilitating the process means having fun.

There are those that believe fun is foolish, fun is a waste of time, fun is a sin. They will tell you that enjoying yourself is the first stop on your trip to hell. I'm not one of them. It wasn't always that way. I had so little fun growing up, I never gave fun gave much thought. That changed one day during a philosophy class at Peabody. The instructor entered. He looked like a mop, dressed like a mop, and talked like a mop. I thought about dropping the course. All of a sudden I was laughing, holding my belly, stomping my foot, and regretting that the class would have to come to an end.

Somewhere along the way he introduced the fact that fun should be an objective. Fun was a means to the end. Fun was an attraction. Fun was a reward. Fun was the lure. He told us to never lose sight of the fact that accomplishment was the goal.

If you want people hooked on your deal, start with a little fun. Gradually you can introduce the pain. They will accept it as long as they know that if they meet the goal the fun returns. If you make the fun, fun enough, it becomes addictive. People will do whatever they have to do to get back to the party. Some of the best leaders I've seen make the environment a ball. Why not? Let people experience Mardi Gras and then explain, if you don't give your all, you'll be asked to leave.

Since I was a kid, I've pursued activities that kept me physically fit. There was a time I was a "no pain no gain" disciple. It worked for me. It doesn't work for everyone. I remember one day in a gym overhearing a woman tell her trainer it took forty-three years to realize she needed to get in shape.

Immediately her trainer identified fifteen exercises that would turn Jello into steel. They started and you could see the pain on her face. The discomfort was evident. It soon turned to agony. They made it through ten exercises and she told him she had to stop. She did and never came back.

Had her trainer understood that if it took that long to get to a gym, her motivation was suspect. Had he had a class from the Mop, he would have understood he needed to change a mindset. That would start by showing her that exercise was fun. Four exercises would be fine. Make them easy. After each set he would give her a Tootsie pop and a foot massage. Once she realized exercise was far more enjoyable than she envisioned, she might buy into it. Once she did he could increase the work load and take her north. He never got the chance.

Facilitating the process means challenging people to be better.

Most people have no idea what they are capable of doing. Circumstances are a wonderful way to show people they are better than they think. History is filled with examples of ordinary people doing extraordinary things. They rose to the occasion. People have stood on top of the Matterhorn and raised their arms in triumph. The same happened on the Eiger, Mount Blanc, Zugspitz, and the Jungfrau. What a terrific achievement. And then there was the guy who did them all in thirty-six hours. He was my hero until I read about the blind man that climbed Mount Everest. Some are puzzled by how performance can reach such lofty levels. I wondered also, but now realize, that the human spirit is incredible and when people are challenged that spirit is ignited. People love to be challenged. They can't wait to be challenged. They need to be challenged.

Think about it. Can you remember any of the people in your life that allowed you to be less? I remember those people that made me struggle. I remember those people that gave me pain. I remember those people that made me sweat. I remember those people that made me hurt.

When I was underchallenged I may have thought it was okay but that was only because I didn't understand the consequences. I didn't know that depriving me of the opportunity to excel was a felony. I don't hold them in contempt because I'm sure they did it out of ignorance.

There was a time when I was ignorant. I remember a terrific athlete. He showed up and did everything better than everyone. What I didn't know was that he was better than anyone operating at 70 percent. I never thought about asking him for more. Had I, we may have gone undefeated.

GET IT UP

In my early years I didn't fully appreciate the link between challenging people and performance. I didn't understand that most people operate at a fraction of their capability. I fell prey to the 110 percent cliché. I would think, if they are giving that much how can I ask for more? My attitude changed one morning as I read the story of a Vietnam Vet who had his legs blown off. To bring attention to a cause he supported, he committed to cross America on his hands. Picture that. He would reach out, lift himself up and place his body back down. At about nine inches per effort he moved his 140 pound torso across the Rockies, Mojave desert, and amber waves of grain. Neither rain, snow, sleet, hail, burning sun, hunger, pain, or loneliness stopped him from accomplishing his goal. Strapped to a leather pad, inch by inch he thumped his way east. Three years later when he arrived at the Statue of Liberty he had concluded his remarkable physical feat.

His effort made me ponder situations where I had asked for more and not received it. At the time I was naïve. I accepted what I got. I figured their tank must be empty. I no longer do. One hundred and ten percent—ridiculous. One hundred percent—forget about it. Eighty percent—I don't think so.

PROOF POSITIVE

The year was way back when. The football season was over and I was on to track and field. I always enjoyed coaching track because of the "one on one" nature of the job. I liked the individual aspect of the interaction between coach and athlete. In between efforts you got to talk about all kinds of neat stuff. Uniforms were lighter and you didn't have to use a megaphone to get your point across.

This particular season I had a talented discus thrower who I believed was better than his performance showed. His distances made you yawn. If you ever got hit in the head with a discus he'd thrown it wouldn't raise a lump. My guy had never thrown the discus more than 115 feet. A major meet was coming up and a newspaper wanted facts. I gave them the skinny. He would be somewhere between 114 and 115. If nothing else he was consistent.

The article came out and they got it wrong. His name appeared and it was predicted he would do 150 feet. At that range he was the favorite. I showed him the article. He liked what he saw. He'd never been the favorite. Not ever. He was an only child and he wasn't the favorite.

I challenged my guy by reminding him he was the favorite. I told him I expected a victory. A smile spread across his face. He said he was going to go get new shoes. He would press his shirt, wash his shorts, put on deodorant and comb his hair. He said he wanted to look good when he received his medal. I told him not to pluck his eyebrows.

His day in the sun arrived. The competition was pretty much doing what was expected. They were all around 115. "The Favorite" was announced. What a challenge. Ernest liked what he heard. All eyes were on "Discus Boy." There was judge in the field who knew Ernest. He was standing at one hundred and fifteen feet, one inch.

Ernest stepped into the circle and launched the disk high into the sky. It went over the judge's head and landed at 147. He blew the competition away. He took home the gold, the girl, and a new attitude.

One way or another leaders find a way to tap dormant energy. If you are looking to get a job done you may not need to hire another person. Just get the three people to pick it up 30 percent.

Facilitating the process might mean you leave it alone.

When I first started coaching track in Roswell, I inherited a great athlete—Leonard Wilder. He was champion pole-vaulter and hurdler. The problem, as I saw it, was that he went off the wrong foot when he vaulted and took too many steps in between hurdles. I made him switch. Soon after, my methods had taken him from twelve to nine feet in the vault and the hurdles became a threat. I was dumb but I wasn't stupid. I told him he could go back to his old ways. He did and set records in both events.

Some things need to be fixed and some don't. If you start to tinker and the tinker doesn't work, put the tinker on the shelf.

Facilitating the process means being consistent.

Hot and cold, wet and dry, in and out, on and off is hard to grasp. The teenage mind has not fully developed and one of its shortcomings is inconsistency. Having a role model that is stable has always paid off. People want to know what you stand for and what you believe in. It's difficult to muster commitment on a moving target.

Facilitating the process means hiring assistants that can teach.

Over the years I've heard the argument that a staff was short handed. I never understood it. There are coaches everywhere. They may not have the title but who cares. Being a coach is not a label but a process. Anyone who can communicate a message can coach. Wendel Swain was a biology teacher and Bill York slept with a slide rule. Both were great. People knew what they were supposed to do and did it.

Facilitating the process means expanding your focus.

There was a point in my coaching career when the here and now was all that mattered. A winning season consumed my focus and was at the heart of my effort. That changed. It might have been the result of a player's success after Yoast, or it may have come from the realization that a football field cannot be seen from space. Sure winning was important but what was so much more valuable were the lessons that competition taught. They were tangible. They were marketable. Those lessons transformed young men and women into productive members of society. The field provided a classroom and that classroom became a bridge to a better life.

Veda Nicely was one of those Blue Chippers that needed a little extra help. As a hurdler she was as good as it got. But Veda was like a lot of young people who have been known to succumb to peer pressure. She was as smart as she was fast and that meant honors classes. Her crowd told her that was the wrong thing to do. Why would you want to study if you could rap on the corner? She was about to take the bait when Bob Atkins showed up. He explained the importance of an education and what it would mean in her life. He didn't put down the rapping thing, he just pointed out it was more fun to rap on a corner you owned. The message got through and Veda excelled on and off the field. She made her way to Bowie State and graduated Magna Cum Laude. Other successes followed. She is now impacting kids in the Prince Georges County school system.

Not every story has a happy ending. Of all the kids I've coached, Tracy Fells was the most likeable. He was an athletic star the day he was born. He was a great young man. His mom had brought him up right and it showed. Whenever Tracy was around, things just seemed to be better. I loved Tracy Fells. In his sophomore year I started to detect a change. He was making a name for himself in football and on the streets. One day I called Tracy into my office and told him I had heard some rumors I didn't like. I suggested he slow down. I pointed out he had a great future and he didn't want to screw it up. I thought he paid attention.

His senior year he brought the Titans another state championship with a remarkable goal line stand. He had a scholarship to Grambling and was destined for the NFL. As a defensive end his instincts were never wrong but as a young man he struggled with finding his way. He liked clothes and the money needed to buy them. He had a new car and a lot of gold. I questioned him about it and warned him again. My input fell on deaf ears. Dealing crack was easy money; $5,000 a day beat flipping burgers. He found out differently.

In 1989 Tracy Fells was convicted of selling narcotics. It couldn't have come at a worse time. The government was looking to send a message. Ten years was normal. Tracy got twenty. He would be the first to tell you he has no one to blame but himself. He knew what was right but chose to ignore it.

When you expand your focus you will be coaching more off the field than on it and for me that just seems right. A winning game pales in comparison to a winning life.

Facilitating the process means building trust.

Trust is the glue that binds husband to wife, father to daughter, teacher to student, leader to follower. If you are going to succeed as a coach you need to establish trust. Young men and women are putting their time, effort, health, and success in your hands. They would like to know that you are a trustworthy custodian.

Do yourself a favor and never ask for trust. Trust is not about words. Trust is about deeds. When you exhibit consistent credible behavior over time, you will be trusted. Don't ask for trust . . . earn it.

Facilitating the process means eliminating fear.

Fear has been around for a long time. Coaches have been addressing it forever. The great writing coach Shakespeare said that "our doubts are traitors that make us lose the good we often may gain by fearing to attempt." How about this: "Fears are thieves that steal confidence and diminish potential." When people are afraid, they don't want to attempt. When someone doesn't attempt, nothing happens. As a coach you have to make it happen and if you have a bunch of fearful people everything slows down.

In 1966 there was a terrific three-sport athlete from a competitive school. He pitched, quarterbacked, and shot hoops. At six feet six inches he was a dominant physical force and anytime you played against him you were in trouble. That was until his father showed up. I'd heard the stories and wondered how he could be dominated by his dad. When his seven-foot tormentor arrived, I had my answer.

There was an instant change. Strikes became balls and touchdowns became fumbles. The reason was obvious. He was terrified with what his dad would do to him if he didn't shine. That fear inhibited his performance. He got away from Dad and went on to have a great college career and became a star defensive end with the Dallas cowboys.

He was always great but when impacted by fear he was less.

Removing fear starts by identifying fear. You'll find it in the eyes. You'll hear it in the voice. You'll see it in the legs. It's born in the mind but lives in the heart. Fear has been known to incapacitate the best. Nothing of consequence has been built on fear.

People are afraid of rejection, failure, embarrassment, change, injury, and a host of other things. Someone may not tell you they are afraid but there will be signs. Look for them. Fear shows up in what people say and what people do. Look for fear in the back of the line. You'll find it with the light on. Once you think you know where the fear resides do something to remove it. People don't like to be afraid. They don't like the feeling of being afraid. Whoever removes fear from someone's life becomes a pal.

Your responsibility is to create a sanctuary of safety. That doesn't mean it will be pain free but it will be injury free—physically and emotionally. Trust will help. If people believe that they are going to be okay and then are, you just scored. Let people extend themselves. Let them eat the forbidden fruit. When they have, and nothing bad transpires, you'll probably see a smile.

Overcoming fear is an energizing agent and when someone realizes that fear was just a four letter word, "dare not" will be replaced by "dare a lot" and then everything goes north.

Facilitating the process means holding people accountable.

I've found in my coaching and teaching career that most people live in the present. They think about the future but for them the future is a fuzzy notion that has little influence on their lives. When someone screws up and you don't do anything about it you send the message that the sheriff doesn't care. To an individual who is prone to temptation you have just given them the key to the chicken coop. And as we all know it's only a matter of time until someone sees the feathers in their mouth. The last few years have shown what happens when people aren't held accountable. I suspect every executive that has gone to jail had been given a pass somewhere along the line. Had they been administered a little justice at the first sign of trouble, their lives wouldn't be in shambles.

MY FAVORITE BIRD

What you might find encouraging is when justice needs to be dispensed it is often the result of self-adjudication. You'll find, more often than not, if you have led people fairly, they will police their own actions. I think it has something to do with human beings having . . . a conscience.

Do you remember the mini-series *Lonesome Dove*? This masterpiece showcased life, death, love, commitment, loyalty, challenge, fairness, and trust. *Lonesome Dove*, in my opinion, the finest movie ever made, was about leadership.

Some people think of it as a cowboy movie. I saw it as two coaches taming the west. While I could probably write a book on the intended meaning of each night's episode, at this juncture I'm only interested in the events surrounding the segment on horse rustling. Excuse me, make that accountability.

Augustus McCrae and Woodrow Call had finally tracked down the bad guys who had been robbing, killing, and burning sodbusters. When they came across the group, much to their surprise, they found their good friend, Jake Spoon, present.

They'd spent a decade as Texas Rangers with Spoon, and their feelings ran deep. Unfortunately for him, their commitment to justice ran even deeper. He pleaded his case by stating he had linked up with the scoundrels as a means of getting through dangerous territory. He explained he had not been a perpetrator in any of the acts, and proclaimed his innocence.

While both of them believed Spoon told the truth, the fact still remained, he crossed the line. As Spoon sat with neck in noose, you could feel him processing that input. Suddenly, he kicked his horse. When I saw it my first reaction was that Spoon initiated the action to spare his friends. He didn't want them to live with the guilt that they had killed their friend. I no longer hold that opinion.

There would have been no sleepless nights. McCrae and Call loved Spoon but that didn't matter. Jake Spoon had crossed the line and it was time for him to pay. He knew it and so he hung himself.

As you go through life you will encounter people that

cannot see the line or choose to ignore it. When it happens you need to do something.

My Roswell football team had made it to the championship. I was not all that optimistic because my star running back had violated some rules and I decided to put him on the bench. Halfway through the game a couple players asked me to let him in. I said no. We went on to win. Afterward, those same two players thanked me for holding firm. I guess it taught them something. The player I punished never thanked me but I got the feeling he understood why I took the action. I don't know how he turned out but if he paid attention to the message I sent, he turned out better than if I'd let him run.

I've found people may not want to be held accountable but they expect to be held accountable. Don't give them a pass. When people aren't held accountable more often than not they get worse.

There are lots of ways to facilitate the process. I've given you a few. In finding others you are only limited by your imagination and a willingness to implement your plan. What is important is that what you do should be measured against one criterion—accomplishment.

Accomplishment is a word with major ramifications. Accomplishment is about being better tomorrow than you are today. Accomplishment involves feeling good about what you did. Accomplishment leaves no doubt that you did your best.

There are many who believe that accomplishment is a point on a performance continuum. For me it has always been a relative term. Accomplishment has nothing to do with where I am. Its significance lies in the distance I've traveled from where I began. If I began great and didn't become greater, great means nothing. There is no victory in maintaining the status quo. Accomplishment has meaning only when it is measured against what could have been, what should have been.

That concept is lost on some. We are living in an age where hype is the coin of the realm. Being provocative makes you a star. When I was growing up, fame and fortune came about as a result of being better than the best. Today, an octopus tattooed on your face can get you front row seats. The nonsense has gotten pretty extreme, but with all things it is only a matter of time before the pendulum swings back.

A MAN TO REMEMBER

I never had a son. I always wanted one. Now don't get me wrong. I adore women. I've spent my life around them and I'm better because of it. Dads and daughters have a special bond but so do dads and sons. More than once I wondered what my son would be like. Had I been able to make one (it takes a real man to make five girls) what would he have been?

I wouldn't have cared how he looked. Short or tall, green hair and pink eyes would have been just fine. Elephant ears and a cauliflower nose, so what. His blood would have been mine. That physical stuff doesn't matter. It's what's on the inside that counts.

My son would have had character and a twinkle in his eye. He would have treated people nicely. And done what was right. My boy would have tackled bias and blocked injustice. My guy would have made a point of speaking his mind. I know he would have wanted to leave the place better than he found it. No, I never had a son but I had Gerry Bertier.

Gerry came into my life when he was in the eighth grade. His father had just died and like anyone who experiences a significant loss, I think he was looking to fill that void. We bonded immediately. I was a kind of surrogate father. Early on I knew there was something special about him. He had a determination and competitiveness that exceeded anything I had seen in someone so young. Not too many thirteen year olds understand realizing your potential tracks back to the present. For most youngsters, here and now is all that counts. For them, success in the future comes on a wing and a prayer. Gerry knew differently. He understood the future began today.

Many young men I've coached are what I call one-linkers. They cannot see beyond the first link in the chain. To a one-linker expending effort means you're tired. Period. That's it. All over. Go home.

To a multi-linker, effort means you're tired.

Tired indicates you did something. Something makes you better. Better wins. Winning gets recognition. Recognition gets a scholarship. Scholarship dictates an education. Education is a future. Future is a good job, a family, and a plasma TV. To a multi-linker tired is not the end of the process, it is the beginning. I can still hear Bertier as if it was yesterday. "Hey coach, I think I'll do a few more laps."

The best athletes and most productive people I have coached never lost sight of the links in the chain. Gerry always seemed to be able to see the connections that others couldn't. And when the links became blurred Gerry had me. That's what coaches are supposed to do—bring clarity to confusion. With Bertier it was easy. Anytime he got off track the solution never required more than a minor adjustment. He was so focused and so dedicated you just had to think the thought and he was on it. He took that attitude to the playing field. He had all the physical equipment needed to play but it was his "don't quit" mindset that made him a star.

I've seen a lot of great plays over the years but one play stands out above all others. We were playing our rival Jefferson. It was tough game and victory was up in the air. Jefferson had a third and long and that was the kind of situation where my linebacking maniac got even crazier. He called his own number for a blitz. At full speed he went through the line like a missile through pudding. He saw the bull's eye and readied to launch the QB into another county. There is one thing about being a legend that can be detrimental. People know your moves. Bertier had a reputation for suicidal aggressiveness. The other coach knew what he would do. A swing pass was called. A moment before Gerry hit his target the quarterback unloaded the pigskin to the fastest man on the field. Bertier hit the quarterback and rearranged his numbers. When he realized the ball was gone he jumped to his feet and ran the halfback down. He caught him at the five-yard line. I guess that meant that guy was the second fastest player on the field. They didn't score and we won the game.

I've contemplated that effort a thousand times. I cannot think of Gerry without picturing that play. It is indelibly etched in my mind. Not because Gerry made the tackle. Not because we won the game. Not because Herman patted me on the back. I remember that play because that play represents the spirit of the man. Of all the young men and women that called me coach, Gerry Bertier possessed a spirit like no other.

As I've gotten older and my past is relived in memories, spirit is always there. I've thought a great deal about spirit. There was a time when spirit came up and I looked to the heavens. I didn't realize that spirit is born on this earth and it is spirit that adds dimension to your life and the life of others. At times I didn't understand the significance of the word. I believed spirit was something you could teach. I no longer do.

Spirit comes in the genes. There are many things that can be learned but spirit is not one of them. From the very beginning, if you have been blessed with spirit you are lucky, because spirit is the pilot light of character. It is spirit that embraces adversity. It is spirit that confronts injustice. It is spirit that overcomes pain. It is spirit that allows a suffering child to smile and a dying soldier to forgive. Spirit said "give me liberty or give me death." Spirit has been at the essence of achievement since achievement began. It was spirit that took Gerry Bertier from the darkest dark back to the light.

A NIGHT TO FORGET

It was December 11, 1971, and Gerry Bertier was on top of the world. The high school heartthrob and hometown hero had just been called the best defensive player in the country. Two hundred schools waited to offer him a scholarship. He was a unanimous All-Metro linebacker and was receiving the

Titans Most Valuable Player award. I was his coach and had the honor of presenting him his trophy.

The audience rose in a standing ovation. As I handed it to him I was surprised by the look on his face. On a night that should have been filled with happiness there was sadness in his eyes. His comment to me was, "Coach, I feel like it's all over." Five hours later Gerry lay crushed in the front seat of his 1969 Camaro after it slammed into a tree a mile from his home. When the doctors finished putting the pieces back together the prognosis was unanimous. Gerry had a 5 percent chance of living. A few weeks later Bertier was alive and getting stronger. The prognosis was unanimous. It would take two years in the hospital before he would be well enough to leave. Six months later he was out. They were right about his never walking again.

In an instant his life had been turned upside down. In the hospital Bertier was given an almost lethal dose of negativity. It was the best thing that could have happened. Gerry was stubborn and he loved proving people wrong. He viewed bad news as a challenge. That's what allowed him to make a remarkable recovery.

But once he got out and realized the struggle that comes with being paralyzed he began to have doubts. A short time later he came to see me. Tears flooded his eyes. I tried to hold mine back. He told me he was going to commit suicide. When I heard the word I became enraged. "Gerry," I yelled, "You were a great football player. You were a great athlete. And you were great not because you had the most talent. You were great because of what was in here." I touched my heart. "And here." I touched his temple. "It was your perseverance, your competitiveness, your never-give-up attitude that made you a champion. What happened to that? Was that killed in the accident?"

He said nothing. I continued, "You're letting what you can't do stop you from doing what you can do." He asked for an explanation. I told him about the Wheelchair Olympics. When I saw a spark in his eyes I knew the pilot light had ignited a flame.

He laughed as he stated he'd have to give up the high jump but then asked if I would coach him in the shot, discus, and javelin. I didn't know my answer would connect us for the rest of his life. I had always accepted my responsibility as his coach and I would again. It would just be on a different playing field.

I'm no different than anyone else when it comes to being clueless. I'd never spent any real time with someone who was handicapped and certainly not at Gerry's level. Nothing worked from the nipples on down. I had suffered with Gerry after the accident as he tried to cope with his new circumstances. I was there to give him a shoulder if he needed it. I attempted to provide some encouraging words. But I never understood what he had to go through until I made that commitment.

Gerry taught me everything I knew about working with a disabled person. It wasn't an easy education. Gerry was known to speak his mind. In the politically correct world we now live in, he would have been a pariah. If a thought found its way into his brain it wasn't long before it cascaded off his tongue. He never ever attempted to sugar coat anything. He was after everybody all the time but only if there was a reason. On occasion he put the "attack mode" part of his personality in neutral and became a reasonable guy.

That happened early on in our quest to win him a medal. It was the first day that we were going to practice throwing the discus. Bertier had worked out in the weight room exhaustively to build his shoulder and arm strength. He was in terrific condition. Remarkably, in that he had no stomach muscles to help him leverage the weights.

Much of what he accomplished was through sheer willpower. He took that same willpower to the practice field. I had positioned myself in front of him and awaited the discus throw. Looking at him you could see the intensity on his face. The frown turned into a grimace and then a maniacal sneer. His shoulders began to rotate as he lifted the saucer into position.

I figured I'd give him some words of encouragement but before I had gotten them out the discus was on its way. What we hadn't factored in was the momentum that allowed the discus to fly also threw his wheelchair over. He landed on his face. I ran over to pick him up and expected a tongue-lashing. With a smile he just said, "Coach, I think you need to hold the chair." From that day on I did. We had great times. Like all competitive people he wanted to win. Frequently he would challenge me. I would climb in his chair and take him on. I always lost, even with stomach muscles.

At the end of practice he would drag himself into his gadget filled car. He'd roll down the window and give me a big grin. "Thanks coach," he'd shout. "I'll see you tomorrow." I can't remember ever looking at him drive away and not feel sad about what had happened.

Bertier could be funny. Gerry never lacked for companionship before or after the accident. His personality was so strong people were attracted to it like a magnet. Many of them seemed to be beautiful. One day Gerry informed me an assistant was coming to help us keep track of his javelin throws. Momentarily, a beautiful blond appeared. We had a tape measure laid out and I told her where to stand. After each throw she would read us the number. Gerry started throwing and she began calling out numbers. I knew they were wrong. I asked Bertier where he had gotten her because she couldn't count. He said he couldn't care less if she could count. He then informed her that I was the math teacher and if it upset me that much, when we finished maybe I should give her a class.

Bertier was an opportunist. At a rally honoring the Titans shortly after the movie came out, I noticed three beautiful women wearing number 42. I went up to talk to one after the ceremony. She told me that Gerry had given her the jersey because she was special. I hoped the other two women left before she found out she wasn't quite as special as she thought.

Above all else Bertier was committed. Until Gerry's accident and my involvement in the aftermath, I never appreciated what many disabled people go through just to live a tolerable life. I never thought about what it would be like to relieve yourself in a sack, take a bath, get dressed, prepare a meal, get around, do a job, find a lover, or have a family.

These thoughts escaped me and I know I am not alone. If you are not disabled you seldom think, "there I go were it not for the grace of God." Thank heaven there are people like Gerry Bertier with a broader perspective.

Gerry was outraged at the lack of consideration for handicapped people in Alexandria. Some have suggested his interest in helping them was self-serving. I can tell you they're wrong. Bertier's wheelchair had become an extension of himself. On a dance floor he could make John Travolta envious. He could do the Twist, Mashed Potato, the Jerk, and all at the same time. Getting around town he could hop up stairs like a kangaroo. No, his interest in bringing help to the disabled in Alexandria transcended nothing beyond doing something right for people in need. Bertier approached that challenge with the same determination that he showed in everything else. He was smart enough to know he needed help and he recruited State Representative David Speck. He took Speck on a tour of the city and showed just how tough it was to get from here to there if you were Gerry Bertier. He didn't let the issue drop. A few years later every restaurant and government office building in Alexandria had handicapped access. The Virginia General Assembly passed a resolution honoring his achievements. As it was read, the entire delegation rose in unison for a standing ovation. No one spoke but everyone knew that they were honoring greatness that ended too soon.

I could go on for a long time telling you stories about Gerry Bertier but I figure you have the picture. People like Gerry are that way because the flame in them burns a little hotter than most of us. And because it does, they find it impossible to live anywhere but on the edge. If they are not walking the wire they feel as if they are missing something. Gerry, more than anyone I had ever met, lived life like there was no tomorrow. On March 10, 1981, at the age of twenty-nine there was no tomorrow. He died in Charlottesville, Virginia, after a head-on collision with a drunken driver.

No, I never had son but I had the next best thing.

THE STORM BEFORE THE CALM

Nineteen seventy-one was the worst year of my life. Surprising in that the Titans had won the title. More surprising was that Herman and I had survived each other. We weren't hanging around together and on Valentine's Day he never sent a card. But we had achieved what we set out to accomplish and in the process had developed a mutual respect.

No, the bad year had nothing to do with coaching. Whoever said misfortune comes in a three-pack knew what they were talking about. It started with Gerry Bertier's accident and then was quickly followed by my discovering Bonnie was an addict. The slide into the abyss had started years before.

It was around the time I caught her playing hooky. It turns out that she was burning incense for a reason. I guess she figured even her clueless dad knew the smell of marijuana. I knew something wasn't right. My gut told me to give her the third degree but I'd gotten tired of locking horns with my teenager. I'd been worn down from years of battles and I'd become a little apathetic. I was wishing and hoping she would just grow up. I guess I forgot I was supposed to participate in the process.

And there lies the fault. My entire coaching career I had confronted transgression. I knew if you let deviant behavior continue it only got worse. I knew this and yet on that day a few years earlier, I ignored the obvious and listened to the vanilla bars that called my name.

I've paid a heavy price for that sweet tooth. Smoking a little weed turned into reefer madness. That allowed the drug demon to search for other highs. Bonnie found pills and a variety of other narcotics.

The conflicts began. The Yoast house became a war zone. Every night that Bonnie appeared was a battle. There were lots of nights we thought she might be dead. The lying and the stealing escalated. Now that I knew there was a problem, I was engaged and that resulted in an endless series of confrontations.

On one occasion Bonnie told me drugs elevated her self-esteem. I countered that drugs were stepladders for fools. She said they made her happy. I told her they would kill her.

One night she came home and told us she had a new boyfriend. She said he was the son of an admiral. We were excited. I knew if you hung around with the right people you would adopt their behavior. What I didn't know was that Frank was a Vietnam vet and an addict. His addictions became her addictions. Things got worse. Nights gone became nights in jail.

Through all of it Betty hung in there. I blessed the day I met her. I thanked God that she was my wife. I also knew that she deserved better. My daughters deserved better. I made the decision to move out. I anguished at the thought but I could see no other solution. If Bonnie was going to destroy herself she would to do it somewhere else. Bonnie and I moved into a small apartment. I remember the night that Sheryl called and asked when I'd be coming home. I wept because I knew the answer.

The torment continued. Tough love became the directive. The admiral's son became a son-in-law. Their addictions consumed them. One night, a few years later she arrived on my doorstep. He was abusing her. I told her to spend the night. She said she couldn't.

A couple hours later she left. A few hours after that her neighbor heard a gunshot. At 4:00 a.m., the son of the admiral put a bullet through his brain. I got a call from the police. My heart sunk as I thought about Bonnie. Had he killed her too? I was relieved to find out she had spent the night at a friend's house.

Frank died but Bonnie's addictions soared. She'd been hanging with a rough crowd and they were happy to have her swimming in their cesspool. It went on for years. Bonnie got pregnant. Who knows what will turn someone around. The responsibility that comes with being a mother did it for Bonnie. She got off drugs. Over the years we revived our relationship. She would bring her daughters over to Bethany Beach and we would have wonderful times. On November 12, 2003, Bonnie died at the age of 52.

The damage done by years of heroin use had destroyed her liver and taken her life.

There is nothing positive about what happened to Bonnie but some good did come out of it. One night after a drug fest in San Diego, Bonnie found herself in jail. I didn't know what to do. My sister suggested that I call my dad who lived in San Diego. She'd stayed in touch. She gave me his number. I hadn't talked to him in forty-five years. My mom had told me he was a bum and my perceptions were a result of her input. What did I know? He had deserted us when I was eight.

Circumstance is a powerful motivator. I got a hold of him and laid out what happened. He said he was on it. He went down to the jail and raised hell. He told the sheriff that his granddaughter wasn't like the hippies that she was with and he believed it was a frame job. Elihu Vaughn Yoast pounded his fist and woke the station. He was just a little guy but he had a bark. He didn't want to sue. He said he'd take Bonnie and get her out of the state. They let her go with the provision she would never return.

That was the start of my dad and me renewing our relationship. It turned out that he was a respected citizen. He was a responsible member of the community. One day when the family was together my daughter asked him if he would like a cup of coffee. When she handed it to him, he handed it back. He politely told her he never drank coffee out of anything but a white paper cup. I don't drink coffee out of anything but a white paper cup. I guess he was my dad and I know Bonnie would be happy that we found each other again.

The journey is a see-saw. It's up and down. It ebbs and

flows. For every high there is a low and every dark cloud is followed by a ray of sunshine. This particular Ray was a black coach named Leathers.

While in the hospital I met his family. He had just received a kidney and pancreas transplant. He recovered from the operation but was having a hard time recovering from the bills that followed. Pat Lovell, the head of transplants at Duke University, called me and asked if I could help in any way. I said sure. The Titans were still in the news so I figured maybe a fundraiser would work. I grabbed a bunch of Titans and headed south. We paid our own expenses. We figured that was the least we could do for a guy who was recovering in the land of Boone. The silent auction was a hit and Ray's bills were paid.

DARKNESS DESCENDS

The date was May 4, 1996, and for me it was an evil day. I hate that day and always will. I despise that day because on that day fate punched a hole in my heart. I knew I would never be the same and I'm not. I never will be.

Death is not an easy thing to accept. When it comes to someone you cherish, and so unexpectedly, it can kill your desire to live.

Just two weeks earlier Sheryl had shown up at my house with her son. She had left her five month old with her husband, Marc. She told me she just wanted to spend some time. That was her way. You never knew what Sheryl might do. Right from the beginning she was the most upbeat kid around. Everyone knew that when Sheryl arrived the happy times would too.

That day was no different. We decided to play a little golf. After eight holes, my grandson Grayson determined he'd had enough. He wanted to go home and selected his mom to be the horse. I protested but Sheryl overrode my decision. She carried Grayson back. I could see by the time we'd arrived she was exhausted. Sitting in the great room she said she felt tired all the time. I figured, like a lot of moms, she was doing too much.

A week later I got a call from Marc. I knew something was wrong because good news seldom comes early. In an instant I was awake. Marc told me Sheryl had just been taken to the hospital. She wasn't breathing. My mind recoiled. I collapsed into a chair. As I sat there, tears flooded my eyes. I could feel my life being sucked out of me one breath at a time. I had to do something but I didn't know what. I got in my car and headed to the hospital. I don't remember anything about that drive. Everything was a blur.

When I arrived, the doctor told me Sheryl was on life support. The look on his face told me her life was over. I couldn't understand it, she had never been sick. It turned out she wasn't. A valve in her heart had collapsed. No history, just a freak accident. I had to see her.

For the next six nights I stayed on a cot near Sheryl's bed. I didn't sleep. At night I walked the halls like a zombie. I was in so much pain. I'd sit by her and look at her face for hours. I'd caress her hand. I'd put it to my lips. God, I was in pain. I was teleported to other places and the memories exploded. I remembered my little girl and the Titans. I could hear her voice shouting for victory. I remembered walks on the beach and days in the park. I remembered wrestling around and throwing the ball. I remembered her senior year when her classmates thanked her for being Sheryl by voting her Homecoming Queen. I had been on football fields all my life but I had never been as proud as the night I watched her crowned.

I remembered our trips to the Kentucky Derby and the one when I talked Sheryl out of placing a large bet on Strike The Gold. He won but she never held it against me. There were so many things to remember. I remembered every moment in Sheryl's presence I was taken to a better place.

The emptiness I was feeling made me sick. I cried and cried and cried some more. I asked myself a thousand times why it happened. I knew the answer. It was time for Sheryl to go. She died that day.

As the funeral procession rode down King Street we passed T.C. Williams. I looked at the stadium stands and I could faintly see the image of a little girl looking back. I knew it was my Sheryl because she had a smile on her face. I wept. An hour later I had buried my pal, my buddy, my love, and my best friend. It was Derby Day.

When you experience such grief, your energy and enthusiasm are destroyed. I decided it was time for me to quit coaching. I spent a year walking the beach in search of answers. I was alone most of the time. My despair was profound. I couldn't shake it. Depression is an awful thing because no matter how much your mind tells you there are others things worth living for, your heart doesn't care.

THE ROAD BACK

One day I picked up the phone and the voice at the other end identified himself as Gregory Allen Howard, a screenwriter. The former Titans were in town to celebrate a twenty-five-year reunion. The papers were filled with stories and that generated chatter. As Greg told me, he had stumbled into a barbershop to get a clip. The room was filled with conversation. A man was talking about the 1971 Titans. He mentioned it was the team that Richard Nixon said helped save a city. Now the difference between people that read the news and those that make it often lies in their ability to see an opportunity. I guess this one slapped him in the face. He began to ask questions and compiled some names. I was on the list. He asked me if I wanted to be a star. He might not have put it exactly that way but when he said Hollywood, I took it from there.

If you've been paying attention, you might have come to the conclusion that I wasn't swinging in the Age of Aquarius. I don't smoke. I don't drink. I don't cuss. Never did drugs. (I'll remind you that I married three beautiful women so I must do something.) I will admit that I'm a low-key guy but that doesn't mean I didn't want to be a celebrity. I'm not talking Tony-Bennett-singing-at-my-birthday-type celebrity. Don't want to paint my nails. I just thought it would be nice to have some of the perks that came with people knowing your name—newspaper in my own yard, mail off the ground, and a seat at my favorite coffee shop. Nothing grand.

At seventy-five I had accepted it was never going to happen. Greg proved me wrong. He invited me to dinner. He told me what he wanted to do. I got excited. I could see my paper landing on my porch.

"Not yet, Bill," he said. Writing the story is easy. Getting someone to make the movie is another issue. He then handed me a contract and $100 to seal the deal. He picked up dinner.

Months passed. I got a call telling me Disney was interested but they would do nothing unless Denzel Washington played Boone. More months went by. Denzel didn't become Denzel by not knowing a good part when he saw it. He said "yes." Will Patton said he would play me. Disney said "go" and Jerry Bruckheimer was asked to bring the magic back.

Right before the movie started to shoot I got a copy of the screenplay. It had one daughter in it. They decided to go with Sheryl because she had been such a Titan fan. Now any parent who has children knows equal treatment is a must. Snub one child, even if it's not your fault, and you will hear about it forever. I saw the script and sweat broke out on my brow. I was a Hollywood newcomer and I didn't know what to do. When I thought about, facing the wrath of three girls that had been raised by Betty Watson, the choice was easy. I told Jerry Bruckheimer a mistake had been made. He explained why the script had been written the way is was and then apologized. Jerry Bruckheimer is a nice man. He said he would have the director Boaz Yakin call my other daughters and explain it to them. He did and everything was fine.

I'll have to admit, the filming of *Remember the Titans* was pretty exciting for me. It took me into a different world. I got to see how movies were made. Boone and I were flown to Atlanta. We were put up in the five-star Henry Grady Hotel. We were given an expense account and told to give it some exercise. I ran mine around the block to a yogurt shop.

Every day a limo picked us up. We were treated like royalty. It made sense. We were "consultants." Herman believed it and took the job seriously. One day during a take Boone noticed that the director had it wrong.

He never carried his playbook in his right hand. He wore his cap at an angle. He noticed other things. The chinstrap was loose. The socks were the wrong color. He began to huff and puff. I could see the agitation. So did Boaz Yakin. He turned to Boone and gave him a smile. "Herman," he said, "it's just a movie." Boone felt better.

I also got to experience what happens when people know your story is coming to the cinema. When you don't have any money, you spend a lot of time listening to the radio. I got hooked when I was in the service. Hour after hour I would listen to anything that took me away to parts unknown. I especially liked music. Porter Wagoner, Patsy Cline, Hank Williams. One day as I was changing the channel I heard a song titled "Diana" by Paul Anka. I soon became a fan. Over the years I'd heard him referred to as a giant among singers, as big as they get. One DJ said Paul Anka was huge. I had images that when he wasn't singing he was dunking for the Harlem Globetrotters. I could see him patting John Wayne on the head.

Fifty years later I was sitting in a restaurant after a TV appearance. Paul Anka walked up. At five feet two inches I didn't recognize him. He introduced himself and as we talked his personality filled the room. He was big, just in a different way. The subject of kids came up. He told me he had five daughters. I told him I had five daughters. We both agreed it takes a real man to make women. We couldn't believe it; between the two of us we had fathered ten girls.

It gets better when the movie is done. It was 2000 and the premier of *Remember the Titans* was front-page news—at least in LA. Disney had spent a lot of money promoting the film and this was going to be a night for the history books. You know the drill. It started by filling up the Rose Bowl with 55,000 groovy dudes. They added five hundred trumpets to the USC marching band. Hot dogs were four feet long and two feet wide. It was a cosmic event. The instructions to the supporting cast were simple. Cheer, stomp, yell, and shout. When the Titans and the stars that played them arrive, you must go insane. The objective was obvious. We want people to think that without the Titans, America was a third-world country. As the producer broadcast what he wanted done, the crowd understood the game. They began to shake, rattle, and roll. The insurance policy was in place. Do what we tell you and you get a party favor. If nothing else, those Hollywood promoters knew something about motivation.

The signal was given and the production kicked off right on schedule. The night became day as a billion watts lit the sky. The limousines that were queued to the Canadian border began to arrive. The stars, starlets, dignitaries, and VIPs exited cars as long as Long Island. They smiled, waved, and strutted their stuff.

As we were introduced the crowd went bananas. People were foaming at the mouth. It's amazing to see what free Milk Duds can generate. I looked over at Herman Boone and his eyes were glazed over. His smile told me everything. It was his moment in time and I knew what he thought. On Samson's best day he couldn't carry his playbook. What Herman didn't understand was people in LA would give a standing ovation to a Pet Rock if it meant a free coloring book.

After a couple hours the fanfare moved to a theater to preview the movie. I stepped out of my limo and the light bulbs flashed. I heard someone shout my name. My chest swelled with pride. I began to fantasize. On Herman Boone's best day, he couldn't carry my playbook. It's dangerous to believe your press clippings. We moved into the theater.

I watched in awe as Will Patton brought me to life. The hayseed had come a long way. The movie concluded to arousing applause. The party moved on. It was a famous shiny place with lots of mirrors. The shrimp were as large as my fist and the caviar was bigger than the shrimp. "Champagne, Coach?" a waiter asked. "No, thank you," I replied. "I'd like one of those pink things with the feather in it." "On its way," he responded. As I looked around the room I couldn't believe the people in attendance. Mickey Mouse was connected. A while later a reporter approached. She wanted some insight. I was feeling a little full of myself. I was going to give her the best stuff I knew. "Fire away," I responded. She popped a question. "Are you and Denzel lovers?"

I'd heard that Hollywood was a different place.

I guess it was.

There was a second premier in Washington, D.C. Sitting in the front row it appeared even the President of the United

States wanted a piece of the action. It was the first time a President had ever gone to a premier. Someone said it was because the movie had cheerleaders. It didn't matter. It was nice to have him on board.

I didn't see much of that movie. Sitting right behind me was Wonder Woman. I spent the two hours peeping at Linda Carter. When the movie ended, the President wanted to get on stage with the original Titans. The Secret Service was having a fit. They hadn't heard that Julius was no longer hanging with the Panthers. It was a wonderful night.

You don't know what other people's lives are like until you get to walk in their shoes. Over the years I heard about what living in New York was like. I read what was required to make ends meet. I couldn't believe it. I didn't believe it. Then the summons came and I was asked to be on *Good Morning America*. The first thing I thought was that I needed to cash a check. I decided $100 would get me to and from New York and allow me to have a night on the town. I figure after seventy-four years of scrimping I'd earned one night of big-time fun. The teller asked me how I wanted my money and I told her to give me five $20 bills. I told her I was going to the Big Apple.

It was the most pocket money I'd ever carried and I was feeling a little like Daddy Warbucks. I landed and a limousine picked me up. I felt I should give the driver a tip. I gave him a twenty and held out my hand for change. He put the twenty in his pocket, looked at my hand and gave it slap. I met the doorman at the Trump Plaza. All I had was another twenty. I asked him for change. He said he didn't have any. I was down to $60 and going south. The bellman took my bag to my room. I wanted to stiff him but I just couldn't. I knew he had family to feed. He was happy to take my twenty. I got into my room and put my money on the table. I hadn't been in New York an hour and my net worth had been cut by 60 percent. I decided maybe I should employ a little "cotton picker" frugality to the situation. I'd get a burger for dinner. I found a deli down the block. Hamburger—$15.95. Coke—$4.00. Apple pie—$7.05. I looked at the check and wanted to leave the waitress a dime for her tip but I just couldn't. I knew she had a boyfriend to feed.

As I was leaving the restaurant I had a panic attack. Did I have enough for breakfast? I thrust my hand into my pocket and pulled out the remaining money. I breathed a sigh of relief. I'd be okay.

The next morning I went and grabbed a menu. I took a peek and decided I wasn't all that hungry. I ordered a coffee—$6.95. I wanted a piece of toast but didn't have enough money. The waitress asked me if I would like anything else. I asked her how much the pats of butter on the table were. She smiled and said no charge. I told her to give me two . . . over easy.

As *Remember the Titans* played in theaters and became one of the top grossing movies of all time, my phone began to ring. People wanted the guy on the screen to be part of the action. I was invited to everything. At a sport trade show in Las Vegas I was given the royal treatment. I sat at my table with a number of VIPs but they were nothing in comparison to the others that filled the room. At one table sat Babe Ruth. In the distance, Hercules and Jim Thorpe were chewing the fat. I looked around to see who else was coming. As my eyes glanced at the entrance my heart began to pound. I was hyperventilating. Venus, aka Cory Everson, the women's world body building champion had just arrived. She had dominated the sport for years and I was one of her biggest fans. Not only could she bench press a house but she also looked great in a thong. To be honest I had a crush. It seemed every man in the room wanted Cory to sit with him. She looked around and approached my table. At seventy-six, your giddy-up is not supposed to get so excited. Mine was doing back flips. "Mr. Yoast," she said. "Do you mind if I sit with you?"

Thank you Jerry Bruckheimer!

TELL ME ABOUT THE MONEY

I didn't want to bring it up. Yes, there was lots of money made and to this day, Disney and gang continue to reap financial rewards. *Remember the Titans* is one of the most popular movies of all-time. And now it's on television, video, cable, and DVD. I heard they were showing it at football camp in Shanghai.

Denzel Washington wanted to build a monument to Boone and me in his courtyard. It turns out he has made more money off that role than anything he has done. I can't guess how many people have a new Ferrari because I didn't get the job. I can tell you there are two that don't.

For years I went to my mailbox looking for an envelope with a Hollywood return address. I knew it would be filled with cash. It never arrived. Remember that $100? At least it was tax-free.

People have asked me if I'm angry about my payday. How could I be? Over the past five years so many wonderful things have happened. I've been given keys to the city, trophies, plaques, and kisses on the cheek. My name is on a barbeque. I've dined with "the beautiful people" and governors know my name. So does the President. A couple parades asked me to be Grand Marshall. The All-American High School East-West Bowl lets me be a coach. But best of all, I've been invited to share my thoughts on teamwork, leadership, and racial diversity across North America. I've been given the opportunity to look into young men and women's eyes and shake their hands.

Someone once said "wealth exists not in what we have but in the fewness of our wants." I want for nothing. No, I didn't get much of a payday and really don't care.

MEAT AND POTATOES

The difference between a life fulfilled and one that missed the mark has nothing to do with scope. I wouldn't have said that in 1939 or 1999. But after examining where I came from and how I got here, my views have changed. As I look back on experiences, a number of things come to mind. First and foremost is that I was always the happiest when I was helping someone else. I can't explain it. There is just something about seeing others succeed that makes me feel better. To be a part of another's success is special. When they appreciate what you have done for them it's even better. There are people who understand it. And because of their existence, others have been allowed to breathe easier. Mary was one of them. She had nothing, but gave everything.

As I've navigated my way I've been taught so many things. I learned that hard work was its own reward, that being proud of what you do makes you proud of who you are, that doing better was more important than becoming better off.

Not long ago I was asked to speak at a graduation. The students were about to shed their security blankets for body armor. I knew they were looking for flowery words and energizing repartee. Heck, I'm a country boy. I didn't have any. I do carry around an action plan that is suitable for any adventure.

Get Prepared. Physically, mentally, emotionally, spiritually. Life is a four-ring circus and you never know what the ringmaster has in store for you. Skill and capability give you options. When you are prepared you control your destiny. I've never met anyone that didn't want to be in charge of what happens to them. Many aren't because they believe opportunity lies at some distant juncture. There is plenty of time to prepare. They don't understand opportunity lives in the moment. Here and now is all that matters. When the invitation to play is extended, it is expected you take it. If you are not properly prepared you'll have to pass. One pass turns into two, two becomes four, four becomes many. Before you know it you've passed on life.

Embrace Risk. There is no adventure in the status quo. If you want a thrilling life, take a walk on the wild side. Risk and reward are inextricably linked. The smart guys understand it. They also know that with failure there is pain and there is hurt. Failure will remove your smile. But failure is seldom fatal, so don't be afraid. Failure is a right of passage. You cannot win if you have not failed and you will not fail if you have not tried.

Dare to Be Different. If the urge arises go against the flow.

Stay Nimble. Flexibility is crucial in avoiding the potholes that come with any journey. The game plan you've created will have to be changed. Count on it and go with it. Staying nimble involves nothing more than recognizing that in all things alternatives exist. More often than not, you'll find the new deal is the deal you really wanted. The *Titanic* was glorious. The *Titanic* was fast. The *Titanic* wasn't nimble.

Play By the Rules. Rules exist for a reason. They protect us against chaos. They might need to be stretched, modified, or bent but they should never be broken. When you break a rule you have established a relationship with dishonor and it's only a matter of time before that association takes you down.

Confront Injustice. Injustice is wicked. Injustice is a slimy, nasty thing. It is an insidious cancer that kills the human spirit. Injustice is a coward that preys on the weak. It is a menacing beast that has never elevated anything and never will. When injustice exists, everything is worse. I hate injustice. It took Raymond Tefteller for me to understand how much. If you want to be on a team that flourishes, be on the lookout for injustice. It will slink into the environment when you least expect it. It may masquerade as a friend. Injustice is friend to no one. Injustice has no right to exist. If you see it, get your gun.

Be Kind. The world is filled with nastiness. Jerks live. There is no need to be one. Some people associate being kind with being soft. I can tell you some of the toughest, most disciplined people that walk this earth are also kind, considerate, and thoughtful. You'll find when you treat people like you would want to be treated, they will treat you like they want to be treated. You help me, I'll help you and together we will get something done.

I've learned some other things in navigating life:

- The natural order does not adhere to your time schedule.
- When the stakes are high, patience can be a liability.
- The best friends are found under the worst circumstances.
- Focusing on everything achieves less.
- There is no greater gift than kindness.
- People are often the inverse of their façade.
- No touchdown has ever been scored on the sidelines.
- Opportunity seldom arrives on schedule.
- People who are unwilling to compromise are on a road to conflict.
- Courage is discounted when the stakes are low.
- Deceit is the frontrunner to disaster.
- Preparation is the first step in turning wishing into winning.
- On the ladder of life, failure is one rung below success and one rung above it.
- Character is not a product of circumstance.
- Overcoming adversity never made anyone weaker.
- When respect is given carte blanche it loses its value.
- Direction without goals is a trip to nowhere.

- Ignorance and temptation are inextricably linked.
- Action is the catalyst for everything.
- Apathy is a curse.
- You will burn up more calories in a two-hour work-out than a lifetime of being nice.
- Greed is the catalyst for gloom.
- Everything is temporary.

OTHER STUFF

On occasion I've been asked how I feel about other stuff.

Appearance. Anyone who does not believe that looking and feeling good are linked probably looks like it.

Ego. A knife that cuts both ways.

Recognition. I've never met anyone that didn't want it. Giving recognition says you are paying attention. Paying attention says you care.

Momentum. An invisible force.

Excuses. Prescription for mediocrity.

Help. When you do something for someone that he or she could do for themselves, you've helped no one.

Adversity. Fertilizer for character.

Honor. Guardian of your self-esteem.

Deceit. Contemptible behavior.

Impulsiveness. Accelerator for bad choices.

Mediocrity. I never knew anyone that wanted to call it home, but many have.

The Inevitable. When dealing with the inevitable now is always better than later.

Loyalty. When it is earned it should be given.

I had very little while growing up but I did have a horse. At least I think he was horse. He had floppy ears, sway back, and knock knees. He didn't go very fast if he went at all. His claim was that he was the only horse ever rejected by the glue factory. He was given to me because no one else would take him. I guess my grand-dad's friend saw "sucker" in my eyes. I called him "Q Ball." As horses go, he ranked a 1 on a scale of 3 to 6. But I didn't care. Q and I got to be pretty good friends. One day I showed up and he was dead. I thought about what I should do. Q had been good to me for the brief time I knew him and as a result he had earned my loyalty. On more than one occasion loyalty has followed people to the grave. I thought he deserved better than having his bones picked clean by a vulture. I went home and got a shovel. I shoveled for two days to get a hole big enough. I pushed him in it and spent another day covering it with chicken wire and dirt. I was crying the whole time. When I finished it was dark so I decided I would sleep next to Q's grave. Every once in a while I think about that lame old horse and the effort I spent on his behalf. And you know what? I'm glad I did.

Failure Starts with a Thought. It's just as easy to think about winning.

Enthusiasm Is Contagious. I've never been in a room where there was only one enthusiastic person.

Risk. The first step toward reward.

The Unknown Zone. The land of milk and honey.

Results. The aftermath of effort.

Drugs. The beginning of the end.

Criticism. A reality check.

WHERE ARE
THEY NOW?

I've always been a spiritual guy. For me that meant whatever happened was supposed to happen. In some ways I've viewed life like a see-saw. It goes up and down but always seeks balance.

The year was 2000 and my daughter Susan Gail was traveling to a concert with her mom. The last time I saw her was 1945. She had never seen me. She didn't know I existed. They arrived at the concert only to find it had been canceled. As they turned around to go home Susan Gail spied a billboard on a movie theater. *Remember the Titans* was playing. She'd heard something about it and persuaded her mom to go. As the two sat there, she felt odd. She couldn't put her finger on it. Her mom said nothing but something in her manner told her there was a connection. Questions followed and answers were returned—"Bill Yoast is your dad." I guess God had a plan. He'd taken one daughter from me but returned another.

If you live long enough your dance card will need a few extra pages. I'm asked regularly about what has happened to players I've coached and people who have enriched my life. Here is the short list.

Barry Etris. Running back on the 1958 Roswell team. Went on to become an accomplished musician and artist. His song "Ruben James" sold 28 million copies. His creations have been recorded by artists worldwide, including Kenny Rogers. His artwork hangs in collections across North America.

Jimmy Locher. Hammond HS guard. He went to West Point and then on to the Harvard Business School. Worked in the White House, the Pentagon, and the Senate. Jimmy served as an Assistant Secretary of Defense in the first Bush administration. Currently works as a consultant and lecturer on Defense. Married his sweetheart and resides in the Washington, D.C., area.

Julius Campbell. 1971 Titan defensive end. Julius attended Ferrum Junior College where a bad ankle injury, which did not heal properly, ended his football career. Julius returned to Alexandria and began his career as an Animal Control Officer, first in Alexandria and then in Prince Georges County, Maryland. Julius still lives in Prince Georges County.

Ron Bass. 1971 Titan quarterback. Ron went on to attend the University of South Carolina on a football scholarship. He lettered all four years and started his junior and senior seasons as quarterback. He was picked as *Sports Illustrated*'s Player of the Week during his sophomore season after gain-ing 211 yards rushing against the University of North Carolina. He is married with kids and lives in Columbia, South Carolina.

Ralph Davis. 1966 Hammond defensive tackle. Ralph went to Old Dominion College. After graduation he returned to Alexandria and built a thriving restaurant business. He now owns four of the finest restaurants in the Washington metropolitan area—The Warehouse, RT's, The Wharf, and The Polo Grill. Ralph lives in Alexandria with his wife, Chris, and their two children.

Kirk Barker. A star on the 1971 Titans, he was also a national rowing champion. He went to the Naval Academy and played football. He received a commission and served in the Navy for five years. He is now CEO of Xtreme Energy. He resides in St. Petersburg, Florida.

John O'Connor. Quarterback of the 1969 Hammond championship team. John was also an accomplished baseball player. He received all ACC honors as a catcher at Georgia. He turned down a professional baseball offer to enter the business world. He is a State Farm agent in Alexandria, Virginia.

Bob Stumpf. Receiver on the 1969 Hammond championship team. Went to the Naval Academy and then on to a distinguished Naval career. At one point he was the commander of the Navy's Blue Angels. He is retired and living in Florida.

Jerry Wilcoxen. Quarterback of the 1958 championship Roswell team. Jerry graduated from Georgia State and became a pilot with Southern Air. He had a distinguished career as a builder in the Atlanta area. He now lives in St. Simons Island, Georgia.

David Sullivan. Football and track at Roswell. Went to Georgia State. Had two successful careers—concrete and communications. He is a community leader in Cuthbert, Georgia.

John Leber. Fullback at Hammond. Went on to Westchester State. Ranked sixth in the country as an AAU wrestler. Majored in crime. Served as a security guard for Amy Carter during the Carter administration. He now coaches swimming and is a Baptist minister.

Lee Califf. Played on the 1969 Hammond championship team. Took a football scholarship to UNC. Majored in political science. Was an aid to Senator John Warner for eight years. Today is director of government affairs with ALCOA.

Keith Burns. Played on the 1987 T.C. Williams championship team. Went to Oklahoma State. Drafted by the Denver Broncos. He has two Super Bowl rings.

Henry Castro. Played fullback on the 1971 Titans. Went to Virginia Tech where he received a degree in architecture. He returned to his native country, Venezuela, and died in a tragic accidental death.

Tom Lewis. 1971 Titan. Tom went into the service and then to the University of Florida where he received a degree in electrical engineering. He is now an engineering manager living in Largo, Florida.

Chris Kusseling. Linebacker on the 1971 Titans. Attended the University of Delaware where he played defensive back. Received his degree in social science and is an analyst with the Department of Commerce.

Steve Guild. Played end on the Hammond and T.C. Williams championship teams. Attended Princeton University and received a degree in art and archaeology. Became an accomplished painter. Passed away in 2003 from cancer.

Steve Borich. Lineman at Hammond. Attended Frederick College on a football scholarship. Received his masters in education from Xavier. Spent thirty-two years in educational administration. Retired and living in Cincinnati.

Charlie Mitchell. Played on the 1971 Titans. Received his degree in music and then became a musician. Played with Bruce Springsteen. Charlie teaches music in Alexandria, Virginia.

I guess this is as good a place as any to come clean. I'm a nobody. Sure, I had success but then lots of people do. I've tried to do the right thing but when I have, I have done nothing more than a billion others. At times I've shown courage. I've also been weak at the knees. I've called a few great plays and punted at the wrong time. When I look in the mirror I see the same face that I saw in Tin Can Hollow. I know the image that looks back is older and wiser but the little boy remains.

And yet I have spent the last few years in prime time. People pay to hear what's on my mind. Some ask for an autograph. Surprising in that my celebrity has nothing to do with me. You've heard my name for one reason; I was lucky enough to have Greg Howard get a haircut in the right barbershop. As a result he put pen to paper and then the actor Will Patton made me look better than I am. Prior to that I would not have shown up on the radar screen of the civil air patrol.

I think there are a couple lessons here. The first is that life's journey is a convoluted walk into the unknown. Hopefully, early on you hear what's important. Better yet you embrace it. Even better, you employ it. And if you do, things will work out. You never know when it will happen. I was eating peanut butter and jelly until I was seventy-five.

The second lesson is that whatever happens to you will be the result of someone liking your story and then doing something about it. It probably won't make it to the screen but that doesn't really matter. What matters is that you like your story too.

When I made the decision to become a "literarian" I was as ignorant as anyone who has ever written a book. I was also as egotistical. I believed my life was special. And why not? Some pretty great things have happened to me. Ego is a powerful force. And it was ego that made me call Steve. The next day he delivered the news.

"Coach," he said. "I just watched *Remember the Titans*. You were on the screen twenty-two times and delivered sixty one lines. We have a problem."

"What's that?" I asked.

"We're short two hundred pages.

The journey had begun.

As I reconstructed my life it became evident that I wasn't so special after all. Supplementing the good was a lot of bad. The warts bloomed. I thought about abandoning the project until it was pointed out that the worth of a story lies in the interpretation of what transpired. In ugly, there are lessons to be learned.

These days I spend a lot of time with myself and the memories that are the tapestry of my life. The journey that was a rollercoaster became an awakening. When I was lost, a helping hand appeared. Whenever I walked in darkness, I was guided to the light. As I look back, I realize I could have done things better. I made mistakes. I have regrets. But on balance, my life has been blessed and because it was, I became better than I ever should have been.

AFTERWORD BY
STEVE SULLIVAN

When Bill Yoast called, I had just reinvented myself. After writing six books I figured it was time to retire my pen. My previous efforts had done well enough that I felt no need to go back to the plate. I wanted to say "no" but I couldn't. I owed Bill Yoast. If he needed me to tell his story I figured it was the least I could do.

That night, as I reflected on the tedium that accompanies book writing, I questioned my decision. I came up with a plan. I would tell Bill that books were passé. We should do a newsletter. Save on time, paper, and postage. People have short attention spans. Six pages were enough. We would just highlight the thrills. Sounded good to me.

Shortly thereafter, I received an email from a fraternity brother who had stumbled across my website. I hadn't talked to him since college. I returned his salutation and asked him about six friends. He informed me that one died at war, another from cancer, a third from a heart attack. He told me the fittest among us had Lou Gehrig's disease.

I was saddened by the input but awakened to the reality that I was mortal. How much time did I have left? A question like that makes you ponder your own journey. I've never met a responsible person that didn't question their existence. Did I do it right? Can I do it better? It's important. For a number of reasons. If you're lucky, you will make it to the rocking chair phase of life. Lots of time for contemplation sitting on that front porch. If you did right, the memories will sustain your final years. Good deeds will deliver flowers in December. On the other hand, if you betrayed a trust, turned your back on a friend or accepted injustice, you will have regrets. GUARANTEED. You will know that you walked the path of least resistance and became less than you could have been. That knowledge will turn summer into a frigid day.

The thought was terrifying.

I decided I would write the book. For selfish reasons. Bill Yoast was my horse and I'd ride him to the finish. I figured, as we dissected his experience, I could take a peek at my own. I would juxtapose one life against another. Bill Yoast would serve as the benchmark to measure myself. I needed my scorecard. I wanted those daffodils.

When we began I had no idea what I would uncover. A two-hour movie doesn't mean you had a life. As the emails were delivered from cyber-space I started to realize that Bill was an original. When I finished with what Bill wanted to say I called Glenn Furman to check on some facts. Glenn wasn't home. I left a message that said nothing more than I needed to confirm a couple dates for a book I was writing about Bill Yoast. Would he please email me the information? Here is his unedited reaction to my request.

Steve,

It was great to hear your voice on the phone. It brought back a lot of good memories of the Admirals.

I was excited for Coach Yoast, when I heard you were doing a book on his life. No one deserves this recognition more than Coach. We have worked together for 35 years and been friends for 41 years.

Everyone that knew Bill Yoast called him "Coach," but his greatest legacy will be about Bill Yoast "the man." Coach Yoast is my best friend and my mentor. He is the person who has had the greatest influence on my life as a teacher/coach and as a human being. He has guided my life in the areas of faith, family, and friends. It can best be said that Coach Yoast is a people person who just happened to be a coach. He is someone that has great compassion, therefore he just continues to give and keep giving.

Bill and I would probably be called the odd couple. He was tall, thin, and blonde. He was the consummate teacher, experienced, mild mannered, basically known as the intellectual coach. On the other hand, I was short, stocky, always talking, hyper, never laid back with my greatest strength being a motivator of young men, inspiring them to achieve above what they thought they were capable of achieving. In retrospect we were probably the ultimate complement for each other.

Bits and Pieces

1. *The greatest lesson that I learned from Coach was that people are more important than wins and losses.*
2. *Success and championships are achieved through people not by a particular system.*
3. *You win through execution and discipline, not by what system you use.*

4. *Everyone in your program is important, not just the stars. Everyone must be treated fairly.*

5. *Select coaches who are loyal to each other and then let them coach.*

6. *Football is a game, so make it fun.*

A Few Stories

1. *Bill's teams were often called the "Dirty 30." T.C. Williams opened in 1965 and Hammond's enrollment was cut in half. Most of the time Bill's teams were totally outmanned but never out-coached.*

2. *Bill and I were scouting opponents for the Washington Metro area regional playoff game between #1 ranked Falls Church and #3 ranked Woodson. It was a great game with the lead changing back and forth. Late in the game Bill looked at me and asked who would you rather play, I said neither one, they are both too good. I asked Bill who would you rather play—he answered doesn't matter, we'll beat either one. Next week we were 3 touchdown underdogs. We won the game 16 to 7. Valuable lesson learned, never again did I enter a game thinking we would lose.*

3. *While coaching the Titans we had the motto, "Titan Pride," which we always would ask the players is that the 'Best' you can be? What a great motivational tool.*

4. *Yes, Coach did have a temper. In 1971 we were going down the stretch to the playoffs needing two wins to make the playoffs. Late in the game we were leading by 6 points. Yorktown was moving the ball through the air. We had a great All-Region quarterback in John O'Connor. I sent John in the game to play defense. He made a play but sprained his ankle. "Coach yelled who put him in the game?" We just looked at each other. Coach did not speak to me until the following Thursday.*

5. *He was also funny. The same team playing Washington Lee, the preseason favorite. They had a 235 pound fullback named Reggie Harrison, later started for the Pittsburgh*

Steelers, for seven years. Early in the game he was tackled in front of our bench and injured his knee. Our team doctor went out, Bill followed him, bent over and said looks too bad for him to continue playing—Reggie did not return to the game. What a break!

6. *While I was head coach at TC we were in a close game at home. We had several former players on the sidelines for moral support. An official's call was made on our sidelines. One of the former players yelled his displeasure at the official's call. The official threw the flag for a costly 15 yard penalty. Upset, I turned and yelled, as was customary for me, "Who did that?" Coach Yoast with his arm around a very scared former player said, "I did Coach." Wow, what a man!*

The greatest respect that I have for Coach Yoast came when I was selected to be the head coach at TC Williams High School. Coach had already completed a very accomplished teaching and coaching career with full honors. He gave me my first coaching job, he was my mentor. When I asked him if he would consider working with me, his answer was, "Coach, what do you want me to do?" I was entering my first ever head varsity coaching job. The program was down, the last 4 seasons no team won more than 5 games. My staff was made up from 2 former head coaches and remnants of 3 former coaching staffs. In a meeting with the TC principal and athletic director, Coach Yoast was asked how long would it take for the untested Coach Furman to turn the program around? Like a proud father, Coach Yoast said, "one year." He was correct the Titans went 8-2-2 and lost the Regional final game on a last second field goal. It was during this 10 year reign that Coach Yoast shinned the brightest. Coach was not only my confidant, the guy that kept everything together, but more important, the father-type image, the counselor, the listening ear, the encourager. When a young man was down and needed help Coach Yoast was always there for them. Bill Yoast made a REAL difference.

Glenn Furman's letter was not a surprise. It was a validation of the man I'd come to know. You've read his story or at least part of it. If you believe that Bill Yoast is a giant among men, think again. If you see him as a god, get new glasses. If you deem that Coach was king, you need to get out more. Bill Yoast is an "everyman." His hopes, his dreams, and wishes are not unique. Neither are the qualities that allowed him to achieve so much. What did make the Coach special was his integrity. He preached it, he lived it, he protected it. Integrity was everything. For Bill Yoast, integrity was not a means to an end, integrity was THE END.

ABOUT THE AUTHOR

Steve Sullivan began his career as an Army Ranger. After leaving the military, he spent twenty years as an executive in corporate America.

He is an internationally recognized authority on sales, leadership, and performance issues. He is the author of two-bestselling business books, *Selling At Mach 1* and *Leading At Mach 2*. *Selling At Mach 1* was a Business Book of the Year selection.

His videos on Selling and Leadership are 1999 Vision Award winners. He has a BA from the University of Florida and a Masters in Systems Management from the University of Southern California.

More about Sullivan can be found at www.stevesullivan .com.

Made in the USA
Lexington, KY
09 December 2018